A Californian's Guide to the

Birds among Us

A Californian's Guide to the
Birds among Us

Charles Hood

Photographs by Callyn Yorke, Charles Hood, and others

Heyday, Berkeley, California

The publisher would like to thank the Durfee Foundation for its generous support of this publication.

IMAGE CREDITS

Andrew Cannizzaro: p. 18 (bottom left, CC BY 2.0) **Jerry Ting:** p. 22 (right), 25 (right), 27 (all), 35 (right), 47 (all), 59 (lower right), 71 (top), 72 (left), 73 (left and bottom right), 75 (all), 76 (right), 80 (top two), 83 (all), 97 (left), 103 (right), 106 (left), 111 (all), 114 (all), 125 (far left), 130 (left), 134 (left), 135 (left), 138 (all), 141 (right) **Callyn Yorke:** p. 25 (left), 41 (lower left), 44 (lower left), 58 (top left), 72 (right, top and bottom), 81 (far left), 112 (bottom right), 113 (top right), 115 (bottom left), 123 (top), 130 (right) **Library of Congress:** p. 66 (top, control number 2014636783), p. 144 (control number det1994000702/PP) **Pacific Southwest Region USFWS:** p. 68 (all, CC BY 2.0) **Susan Young:** p. 85 (right) **Benjamin Balázs:** p. 87 (left) **Joshua Tree National Park:** p. 109 (top) **Mike's Birds:** p. 119 (left, CC BY 2.0) **Emilie Chen:** p. 119 (right, CC BY 2.0) **All other photos by Charles Hood**

Library of Congress Cataloging-in-Publication Data

Names: Hood, Charles, 1959- author.
Title: A Californian's guide to the birds among us / Charles Hood ;
    photographs by Callyn Yorke, Ph.D., Charles Hood, and others.
Description: Berkeley, California : Heyday, 2017. | Includes index.
Identifiers: LCCN 2016050866 | ISBN 9781597143837 (pbk. : alk. paper)
Subjects: LCSH: Birds--California. | Bird watching--California.
Classification: LCC QL684.C2 H587 2017 | DDC 598.072/34794--dc23
LC record available at https://lccn.loc.gov/2016050866

Cover Photo: American crow, photo by Charles Hood
Cover Art and Design: Ashley Ingram
Interior Design/Typesetting: Leigh McLellan Design and Rebecca LeGates

Published by Heyday
P.O. Box 9145, Berkeley, CA 94709
(510) 549-3564
www.heydaybooks.com

Printed in East Peoria, IL by Versa Press, Inc.

10 9 8 7 6 5 4 3 2

Dedication

Charles Hood: I dedicate this book to Jared, Amber, and Nick-Jack. Thank you for singing the Lawrence (of Arabia) Goldfinch song with me at Morongo, for eating gallo pinto for breakfast in Costa Rica, and for not minding when we left the car in the middle of the road in Hawai'i to chase that tropicbird over the lip of a volcano.

Cal Yorke: I dedicate my contributions to this book to all instructors of natural history, along with their students and their descendants; to my mentor, the late Dr. Howard Cogswell, who provided the academic foundation for my field studies in California; and, above all, to all of my students, past and present, who helped create the teachings we shared.

Contents

Introduction

*Once upon a time, when women were birds, there was the simple
understanding that to sing at dawn, and to sing at dusk, was to heal
the world through joy. The birds still remember what we have forgotten,
that the world is meant to be celebrated.*
—Terry Tempest Williams

Why Watch Birds?

Well, why not?

So there you are, inching up the Bayshore Freeway between SFO and the late, great Candlestick Park, or standing in line at the San Diego Zoo, or maybe waiting for chorizo and eggs at a beachfront Santa Monica café. You're stuck anyway, so why *not* watch birds? Because they certainly are out there: hundreds of species in streaming flocks. May as well watch them. What else is there to do?

And we have to admit they are flat-out beautiful, or most kinds anyway. We sometimes take birds for granted because we see them in parking lots or scratching around under the oleander, but the best-looking ones really are off-the-chart fabulous. Worth a stare or two, a tufted puffin or bald eagle, and a stare-and-a-half, the yellow-billed magpie. Related to crows and jays, this oak-and-savannah bird is a California endemic (that is, found no place else) and has the attractive habit of posing at roadside rests along 101. It has a bill so yellow it looks as though it's been painted on with enamel, and the feathers in the sunlight glow blue, green, neon black. Tanagers and orioles, hummingbirds and warblers: a bird guide is one long parade of wow, wow, wow. Even the truly ugly birds—the head of a condor comes to mind—can still help the rest of us feel less like day-old oatmeal.

> *Birds are holes in heaven through which a man may pass.*
>
> —Jim Harrison

Top: A yellow-billed magpie at a rest stop on Highway 101.

Black-footed albatrosses breed in Hawai'i and cross the Pacific to California's offshore waters.

Above: Tufted puffins nest on the Farallon Islands, just 28 miles west of the Golden Gate Bridge.

Cliff swallows swarm under I-5; they use saliva and mud to build nests.

It's an easy hobby to have because it never goes on strike or has a bad season, and all parts of the state offer great possibilities. There's never a month in California when some kind of bird activity is not taking place. From Arcata Marsh to the Desert Studies Center at Zzyzx, birds are everywhere. Even the grim monotony of I-5 is broken up by swarms of cliff swallows nesting under the bridges or the sudden dives of hawks swooping down on jackrabbits. If you go on a whale-watching boat in Monterey in summer, besides gulls and more gulls you can see albatrosses and shearwaters, plus sea otters and blue whales. Hiking in Sequoia National Park, walking to class at Humboldt State, riding a ski lift at Lake Tahoe? Birds and more birds. Even our largest cities generate impressive lists. A midwinter survey of a ten-mile circle centered on San Francisco tallied 186 species of birds in one twenty-four-hour period; weekend counts in Los Angeles County in spring can top 270 species. In two hours of careful observation, 50 bird species may be found within a 0.1-mile stretch of the Willow Street shallows of the L.A. River during fall migration, without either the bird's or birder's feet losing contact with the concrete.

Imagine what might happen if birds studied us.
—Noah Strycker

Birds use many things to line their nests, including lint, kapok tree floss, and human hair. This mountain chickadee is plucking fur from a dead mouse in Yosemite.

And then there's all the crazy stuff birds are doing all the time. Take swifts, for example. Black swifts nest behind waterfalls; another party trick is that swifts only mate in midair. Like winners on an episode of *Fear Factor,* great horned owls eat everything from porcupines to eels to scorpions. The American kestrel—a small, buoyant falcon—can catch bats in mid-flight. An albatross can fly for weeks on end without landing; it can drink seawater, extruding the excess salt out a tube on the top of its bill. To get rid of feather lice, some land birds practice anting. That means taking a dust bath in an ant colony, letting the ants climb on them, and then crushing the ants with their beaks and combing their feathers that way. The formic acid from the ants repels parasites.

All of this happens in plain sight: once you start studying birds, it only takes a week or two before you starting going, "Huh, I never knew they did *that*."

Is it true that some of us might be happier if we were birds? Not just so we could fly (everybody wants to do that), but what about the lessons we can learn from the humble pinyon jay? It breeds in communal flocks and lives in the sage-and-pine steppe of eastern California and the Great Basin. This jay forms complex social groups in which siblings and aunts help raise family members—a perfect model of extended family and communal support. For food, its vegetarian livelihood depends on stashing pine nuts, and a single bird can remember the exact locations of thousands of cached seeds, even after snowfall covers the ground. In contrast, most of us would be happy to remember what we changed our password to, or where we last set down our coffee mug.

As totem spirits, mythic animals, and even liturgical heroes, birds inhabit our dreams and religions. The raven appears in Norse mythology as well as Middle Eastern traditions; weddings and peace ceremonies release doves (some of which are promptly eaten by hawks). Northern flicker feathers add color and structure to Native American basketry. A review of birds in literature could (excuse the pun) fill a book—several books, actually—with a special chapter set aside just for Shakespeare. From skylarks to woodcocks, more than sixty bird species populate the Bard's plays and poetry.

One story has it we flew in here on the backs of birds.—Tom Crawford

On an ecological level, birds can link us to grander realities, and they help us connect one part of nature to the next. Learning about birds encourages us to learn the names of trees, track which plants are in bloom, or notice when the jet stream is about to swing south and scatter snow buntings across Point Reyes like a hailstorm of sparrows dressed in white dinner jackets. There is always something to notice; birds open our eyes and our hearts.

What Is a Bird?

A bird is a dinosaur—and in the case of an emu or ostrich, birds today can be much larger now than their therapod ancestors. Most birds have hollow bones, highly efficient hearts, and lungs with more capacity, pound for pound, than a track star's. All birds have feathers, even penguins and New Zealand's kiwi, a flightless bird whose feathers look like shaggy fur. A woodpecker's stiff tail feathers prop it up while it jackhammers tree bark to dig out tasty grubs. Feathers insulate, provide lift in flight, attract mates, repel water, line nests, and confuse predators. *Birds of a feather flock together* the old expressions assure us, while a corrupt politician *feathers his own nest*. Success on a project gives you *a feather in your cap;* with luck you did not have to *ruffle too many feathers* to get the work done.

The specifics of plumage vary by body size and how waterproof things need to be. The petite hummingbird has only 1,000 feathers, while swans wear 25,000. Even though they

Above: Daily grooming is called preening, which is what this American goldfinch is doing.

Right: This turkey vulture's ragged shape shows that it's mid-molt.

In six thousand years, you could never grow wings on a reptile. With sixty million, however, you could have feathers, too. —John McPhee

are a miracle of tensile strength and weight, feathers do wear out: molting means a bird is replacing some or all of its feathers. Most birds in our region molt twice a year, before breeding and after. If you look closely, you can often see old and new feathers on the same critter. Many larger flying birds like hawks and ravens show a gap in the edges of their wings where a feather is growing back in. You may even have found some of these dropped feathers while out hiking—they are love letters to you from the sky.

There are about 10,000 bird species worldwide, though the exact total varies slightly from expert to expert. You may also see that in some field guides they list names in alternate formats, so that what is a mourning dove in this book (lowercase) sometimes gets styled as Mourning Dove,

There are eight species of pelican worldwide, all similar in shape. This basic body plan has remained stable for 30 million years.

I often think of the Paul Valéry remark, "To see is to forget the name of the thing one sees."
—Linda Connor

initial caps. That usage follows the quirky rules of professional ornithology, so bird names often get spelled and hyphenated in arcane ways: in the rule books, the twice-hyphenated name "Black-crowned Night-Heron" is correct, even if most English teachers would type it differently. Furthermore, British English varies from American English. What we call a merganser (a kind of duck) is to them the goosander, and our common loon is a harbors-and-lakes bird they know as the great northern diver.

Related to names and spelling is the problem of how to order the entries themselves. Some bird books organize contents by color and others by size or by habitat. Most use taxonomic relationships, so the oldest lineages come first. This sequencing used to mean that the loons, originally thought to be the most primitive living birds found in North America, came first, but now we have refined that idea and the goose family takes priority. Hawks come in the middle, as do woodpeckers and parrots. Warblers and finches come at the end. These ideas are still being developed, and if you compare recent field guides to ones published even ten years ago, you'll see the group orders

Named after a British flycatcher, the American robin is really a thrush.

have changed. Taxonomy (the nomenclature that explains nature at the genus and species level) and systematics (the study of evolutionary relationships among groups) are vibrant, exciting fields. That means that in future bird books the relationships may shift again as DNA research and fossil discoveries help scientists more clearly understand evolution's twists and turns.

Bird names sometimes change too, for example when one widespread species gets parsed into finer units. This is called splitting. (When two become one it is called lumping.) If you keep numeric tallies of your overall sightings, splitting is great news. Local chambers of commerce love it too. North America used to have just one kind of scrub-jay, but now officially we have four: one in Florida, two in the American West, and one found only on Santa Cruz Island off the coast of Santa Barbara. Each has its own common name (the usual term most people use) and its own Latin name (the two-part scientific name unique to each species).

The wrens' invisible looping their loop—
And I, for a moment, pinned to the ground.
Pinned and spinning in the sound of it.
—Laura Donnelly

All names (common and scientific) used in this book were current as of press time, and every bird and place mentioned in the text has been cross-listed in the index.

How to Go Birdwatching

Get up early. Put on your softest, quietest clothes. Step outside.

More or less, that's all there is to it. Being up early helps but is not always essential—most of the pictures in this chapter were taken in the middle of the day. Drab clothes help (birds can see in color and have remarkable "zoom power" vision) but don't matter all that much, especially not in areas with lots of people already. A jaunty hat helps keep the rising sun out of your eyes. Unless you live in a house overlooking Bolinas Lagoon, getting outside helps, though in some marshlands your car can be the best hideout. Otherwise this is a walking hobby and the more you're outside, the more you will see. Bring binoculars if you have them.

Being quiet helps a whole lot—turn off your phone, leave Old Yeller at home, and just try to take in the total environment, including what you hear, what you smell, what is going on overall. Walk slowly and stop often. Look up. Look behind you. The single biggest mistake most nature novices make is chatting too much. That includes the "Oh, how pretty!" running commentary, as well as longer, non-bird-related stories. Some folks never seem to stop talking from the start of the trail to day's end, and they inevitably will see fewer birds…as will everybody stuck near them.

Most chapters of the Audubon Society offer monthly bird walks (usually free), as do many nature preserves. All of these groups welcome beginners. When getting started, a bit of guidance helps; don't be shy, go out often, and always ask a lot of questions.

Do I Need Binoculars?

Oh, jewels and binoculars hang from the head of the mule. —Bob Dylan

Eventually everybody spending any time outdoors wants binoculars, and as with the toys for any elite hobby, there's always the next model up you covet with all your heart. Be prepared for sticker shock, since top-end binoculars cost thousands of dollars.

The good news is there are bargains for much less than that, and if you ask around, somebody you know probably has a pair they are no longer using, and free is the best price of all. Numbers on the different kinds will come in forms like 8x30 or 10x40. The first number is magnification (less than 5 is not much help, and more than 10 is too hard

"There, *that* one!" Birdwatchers study gulls and shorebirds along the L.A. River.

to hold steady), and the second number is the size of the big end of the glass, measured in millimeters. Avoid most zooms and autofocus options and just get the kind you focus yourself. Online forums debate the merits of this or that brand with more scrutiny than wine magazines ranking merlots. The bottom line is that if you're buying them, get the best glass you can afford, and if you're borrowing them, be sure to say thank you.

Where Should I Go?

Interesting places for vacations—Yosemite, Big Sur, Catalina Island, Joshua Tree National Park—are almost always interesting places to go birdwatching. Most state and federal parks have printed checklists at the visitor center or entrance kiosk, and most sites have sightings listed on an online database called eBird, which is introduced in Appendix II. Looking for stops to check for birds will help break up travel days and help you find a picnic spot you might not otherwise suss out.

One reason we have so many good options is thanks to the state's physical and botanical variety. The more habitats a region has, the more different birds there will

be. Altitude helps too. Mount Whitney remains king of the Sierra, with a recalculated height of just over 14,500 feet. From the summit, with X-ray vision (or a vivid imagination) one can look down at Badwater in Death Valley, 282 feet below sea level. With so many microclimates and so much corrugated topography, California has more native plant species than the eastern US and Canada combined. Meanwhile, a vast jungle of urban trees turns our cities into semitropical botanical wonderlands. All those plants guarantee that we have a diversity of wildlife to match.

Contrary to the clichés about concrete wastelands and the zombie apocalypse, California is a great place to be a bird. Nature thrives here. From mockingbirds to parrots,

When it's over, I want to say: all my life
I was a bride married to amazement.
—Mary Oliver

Top: Hammon Grove in Yuba County is a good example of a riparian (streamside) habitat.

Center: Yosemite National Park has a species list of 265 birds.

Bottom: Antelope Valley is an hour north of Los Angeles. Come for the poppies, stay for the hawks, falcons, vultures, owls, and eagles.

The Salton Sea is a surreal 35-mile-long lake created by accident 100 years ago. Hardy birdwatchers check here for blue-footed boobies, stray seagulls, and desert species like Gambel's quail.

bald eagles to bluebirds, this state is bursting with bird species—673 different kinds as this book goes to press, twenty more than Texas and a list that grows by one or two or three new species each year. (No state in the US has a higher overall total.) Redwoods, grasslands, deserts, beaches: each of these habitats has its own unique bird communities.

Of course, some of the other places that are good for birdwatching probably won't rate so high on the family bucket list.

This includes the hallucinatory shores of the Salton Sea, Death Valley in the hotter months, landfills (when you can get into them), cemeteries, sewage ponds, desert washes filled with shot-up signs and abandoned cars, and the concrete-lined Los Angeles River. Birds don't worry about postcard views: they just need the same things any animal does, including food, shelter, and a fighting chance against competitors. In nature, untended and feral usually offer more options than tidy and clean-edged. If the best feast of aquatic insects is in a freshwater marsh, then migrating shorebirds will chow down there. But if there is no marsh and insects are more easily found in the algal mats of the L.A. River, the dunlins and curlews and phalaropes will ignore the shopping carts and storm drains, and shift to urban Long Beach instead.

The great blue song of the earth is sung in all the best venues— treetop, marsh, desert, shore.
—Sidney Wade

Birdwatchers versus Birders

A bad day of birding is better than a good day of work.

The words seem so similar, "birdwatcher" versus "birder." After all, if a birdwatcher is somebody who watches birds, why create a second term? A birder watches birds too, but with a greater intensity than might seem healthy or normal—longer hours, farther drives, pricier binoculars. Another difference is that birders keep lists. There can be so many: a year list, a yard list (all the species ever seen from your property), a county list, a world list, a seen-from-the-train-on-the-way-to-work list. Each new bird checked off the list is like a hit of a strange and magical drug. There is an added pleasure when one gets a new bird that a rival doesn't have. And it is a lifelong project, since one's list never ends. Nobody has seen all the birds in the world, and in California, the vagaries of weather and the times a migrant's internal compass goes kaplooie both can coincide, so out-of-range strays can turn up anywhere. The California bird list includes species that show up once a year, once a decade, or maybe only once ever. There is always something new to see.

All of this includes a dial-a-friend component. If a mountain bird turns up in the lowlands or a Siberian finch makes a wrong turn at the Aleutian Islands, once it has been spotted the alerts flash out like NORAD scrambling F-16s. Coffee splashes into travel mugs, car doors slam, tires spin, and the chase begins. Will our plucky birder get there in time? You may only get one chance. Some stray birds are cooperative, even patient—they may settle into their new zip code for weeks on end. Others just stick around an hour, maybe half a day, and then take off looking for a better deal elsewhere.

Once you reach the right marsh or patch of cottonwoods and dash up to see your target, that's it. There is no further verification. Did you see it yourself? Was it alive and unrestrained? Did you identify it with certainty? If you can answer these questions with a string of yeses, then congratulations. It's on your list. No photos required: your word of honor will be good enough. Birding is one of the last chivalrous sports in the Western tradition. Cheat on your list? Unthinkable. The shame and guilt would be too much to bear.

Listing is fun, and for some, fiercely addictive. Yet the size of one's list has little to do with how good one is or isn't at birdwatching, and lists are even less useful when predicting how much pleasure one finds in studying nature.

As Lynn Thomson says, "Some people are very competitive in their birding. Maybe they'll die happy, having seen a thousand species before they die, but I'll die happy knowing I've spent all that quiet time being present."

Natives versus Exotics

A bird is a bird is a bird, except when it isn't. Some people make distinctions based on origins. Pigeons, starlings, house sparrows, collared-doves, or the parrots of Telegraph Hill: all of these arrived here from elsewhere.

Figuring out origins can be tricky. Turkeys are native to North America but not to California—they were released here as a game bird, to provide stock for hunting. (Wild turkeys are cannier and stealthier than the barnyard kind, and are harder to stalk than one might guess.) Another California bonus bird is the pheasant, native originally to Asia. Yet it comes to the United States courtesy of Great Britain, having first arrived there with the Roman legions. We could label it a Chinese bird, a Roman bird, or

Starlings are common—and commonly reviled. Yet if they only showed up once a decade as windblown strays, birders would drive all night just to see one.

maybe just an Austin Powers bird—please meet the ring-necked pheasant, international man of mystery.

This all means that in a lunchtime visit to a city park, most birds you might see are technically "non-natives," a group collectively called exotics or introduced birds. Historically, their ancestral stocks were not found in North America. Of course, if we pull the camera back far enough, that is true for all of *Homo sapiens,* too. All of us—even Native inhabitants—came to the Americas from someplace else. On a geological scale, the Paleo-Eskimos barely got here before the Spanish brought the horse back to North America and a man named Eugene Schieffelin released the first European starlings, stupidly planning to populate America with all the birds mentioned in Shakespeare.

Even native birds like seagulls have had massive population explosions and range expansions due to man's alteration of the environment, and in San Francisco and Los Angeles, the once strictly coastal western gull is now regularly much deeper inland than it was even fifty years ago. Are coastal gulls "native" to Burbank Airport? They never used to be, but they are certainly there now.

The fact is that all of us now inhabit a blended ecology, plural and comingled, and any yearning for a lost or pure pre-Anglo avifauna is mere nostalgia. Still, the bias runs deep. Native birds are legally protected, but non-native birds can be shot on sight. Maybe instead of being cursed as pests and carpetbaggers, the exotics should be praised for their ability to survive. Roger Tory Peterson, the father of modern field guides, said it best: "I admire the house sparrow, because it's a bird that manages to live on our terms, and we're the most difficult animal in the world."

The One That Got Away (Plus a Note on LBJs)

Nature is the endless infinity. —David Hockney

Irritating but true: some birds you come across won't match the illustrations on any page of any book. That's normal. After all, the world is a strange and inexplicable place. Sometimes food can stain a bird's face pollen yellow or blackberry purple. Genetics misfire: an albino bird is white, a leucistic one is mostly or partially white, and melanistic means blacker than usual. In gulls and ducks, hybrids (a mama of one kind, pappy of another) blur the usual boundary lines. A glut of light can play tricks on us, or an odd molt can leave things blotchy and askew. And of course in birds as in people, juveniles can look (and act) truly bonkers.

Nobody can identify all the species all the time, and more than once you are going to end up on a boat trip or group walk and the leader at the front is going to announce with confidence, "Look, a such and such," while in the back, not having heard the first chap, the other leader will name it as something else entirely. The world is mysterious; not everything can be known; experts mess up. A certain amount of confusion is inevitable.

One bird, two postures: two great egrets show how different the same species can look.

Eating a coot, this juvenile great horned owl looks like it just raided mom's closet. In a few months adult plumage will grow in the rest of the way.

Crescents around the eye help identify MacGillivray's warblers. The name honors a Scottish naturalist who once walked from Edinburgh to London just to examine a bird specimen.

One abbreviation can be handy here. LBJ, in ornithology, means not President Johnson (whose wife, you'll recall, was Lady Bird), but Little Brown Job. British birders use that expression too: it means drab and smallish, the kind of sparrow-y, warbler-y item that could by any one of a dozen species. LBJs are especially likely on trips when you're starting to learn your birds fairly well and decide to take your out-of-town relatives to your favorite local marsh or forest. Instead of western tanagers or breeding-plumage avocets, you are almost guaranteed to run into nothing but flock after flock of perplexing LBJs. "What's that one?" they will ask helpfully, pointing to the mystery bird perched in clear view of everybody. "Um…"

The worst part is that you're probably going to figure out what it was hours later, just as you start to fall asleep.

How to Use This Book

This book will help you identify 120 birds commonly seen in the inhabited parts of California, with a few aspirational species like the vermilion flycatcher added for zest. (You really want to see one of these, but may not know it yet.) Not included are specialty seabirds, high-mountaintop birds, or multiple examples of a given group. Half a dozen of California's forty-plus duck species are reviewed here—the ones you're most likely to notice as a beginner—but the rest are not. There are just too many to fit into an introductory guide. As your skills sharpen and your list grows, you may end up getting more detailed books. Suggested titles are listed in Appendix I.

One way to begin learning birds is just to flip through the pages, stopping when a name seems familiar or a profile triggers a memory—"Oh, so *that's* what you call those crazy ducks in the park." This book intentionally pays less attention to LBJs and more to the large, obvious, clearly "seeable" species you're most likely to come across. These are indeed the birds among us, and this book offers a very attainable survey. If you wanted to, you could see every species in this book in less than a year.

It may sound counterintuitive, but learning birds is less about colors and field marks and more about general size, behavior, time of year, and habitat. A barn swallow seen backlit against the sun may appear entirely black, but when seen from another perspective, it has a cinnamon belly and stunning midnight-blue back. Yet in any light, the shape of the tail won't change, nor will its looping flight style. Even if you don't know *which* swallow it is, once you start to learn the general categories of size and behavior, you can tell it is a swallow and not a flycatcher or baby hawk, no matter how tricky the lighting.

What that means is when you see something you're trying to figure out, start with some ballpark guesses. Luckily you have a lot of general impressions already. Those will help you narrow things down. Is it sparrow-sized, or more plump and hefty (robin-sized), or something as big as a duck, heron, or hawk? What's it doing—soaring? Waiting attentively on the tip of a branch? Or perhaps zigzagging along the edge of an estuary and jabbing its bill up and down as rapidly as a sewing machine finishing a hem? Most birds find food in predictable ways, and that behavior helps aids identification. Kingbirds sally from perches; sparrows hop and peck; kingfishers plunge headfirst into rivers like air-to-sea missiles.

Bird populations change each year. Originally a pet-trade bird, the scaly-breasted munia lives in marshy fields from San Diego to San Jose.

Field notes don't have to be elegant or complete. The black butt helps confirm that this bird, studied at Malibu Lagoon, is a gadwall.

Studying birds often leads to other pleasures, like noticing dragonflies or discovering that lesser long-nosed bats raid hummingbird feeders.

The calendar helps as well. Hard-core birders chase random strays, but most birds end up where they belong, and do so more or less on schedule. Some birds breed in the tundra and winter in South America, following the Pacific Flyway as they migrate through California. That passage happens in a fairly predictable pattern, so timing can help with identification. With some shorebirds, for example, southbound migration is already underway by late June and early July, and as you learn the ebb and flow of arrival dates, that makes sorting things out a lot easier.

Sketching a quick picture can be fun and helpful, as can taking a few notes. What may seem obvious at the time will probably fade and blur once you get home and try to recollect your day. "Wait, was the black line through the eye or was it more like a stripe on top of the head?" "Was the beak curved or straight?" As Harvard's Louis Agassiz used to say, "A pencil is one of the best eyes." Henry David Thoreau's fame as a naturalist comes as much from his journals as it does from his classic memoir *Walden;* Roger Tory Peterson trained himself to observe closely by sketching in the field.

Drawing shorebirds will train your eye to capture the subtlety and nuance of shape and the contrast of size.
—John Muir Laws

Reading this book ahead of time certainly will help you ID things more quickly in the field, but the best thing to do is just to go out and look at birds. Have you ever tried to learn a new language? Most people find sitting down with instructional tapes less fun than putting language into action by watching *telenovelas* in Spanish or trying to order off-menu in Quebec. You get good at any new skill by jumping in and doing it, so the best way to use this book is to stick it in a backpack, lace up your trail shoes, and just go out and see what you can see.

Bird Species

A great blue heron stretches its wings in a city park.

Snow Goose *Anser caerulescens*

 marshes, fields, city parks (sometimes)

Smaller than Canada geese, our local snow geese are almost always white with black wing tips, and with pink feet and bills. In wildlife refuges around Sacramento and the Salton Sea they fill the sky with ribbons of white. A few show up in winter parks, becoming in-betweens: not quite tame, not quite wild, and seemingly still trying to decide which identity to go with.

Just to keep beginning birdwatchers alert and humble, somebody invented a look-alike species: the Ross's goose. They look almost the same, though it is slightly more likely to be a park duck than a snow goose. The usual description is that Ross's has a shyer, more bashful air to it, is smaller, and has more of a snub-nosed beak. Everything on the Ross's feels more rounded and compact. Most rare bird alerts will track a Ross's if it's in town, though updates at the end of the winter may taper off. In addition, some snow geese march to the beat of a different drummer and are blue-phased all their lives; that's less common here than elsewhere in North America. Our default snow goose color is white as snow (or at least white as dirty snow).

Nesting in Canada and Alaska and wintering in California, Texas, and Mexico, their population grows yearly; nationwide there may be 8 million. Not all are here, but it can look like it some days. If you want to experience a million waterfowl at once, plan a trip to the Lower Klamath Basin in winter; Sacramento National Wildlife Refuge is another great choice and is just a few minutes east of I-5. (It has snow geese in summer as well.) In the south, fields around the Sonny Bono Salton Sea National Wildlife Refuge add another 30,000 birds to the state's winter total. Yes, it is named after *that* Sonny, and it seems like unfinished business that we've not yet found a lagoon or county park to name after Cher.

One swallow does not make a summer, but one skein of geese, cleaving the murk of March thaw, is the spring.

—Aldo Leopold

In California, snow geese (above and top right) are almost always white with black wingtips. The Ross's goose (bottom right) looks like the snow goose but is always smaller.

Canada Goose *Branta canadensis*

🔭 marshes, fields, golf courses, city parks

Everybody liked Canada geese better in the old days, when they formed classic V formations and honked their way north each year. Now they pick a park or golf course and move in permanently. By staying put, they clip the grass short (good) and look noble and scenic in their serene flotillas (good), but leave a mess of droppings (bad). Thick smears of goose poo muck up the path, spreading disease and making it hard to walk. Once in a while an overly territorial goose nips a jogger. The US Airways plane that belly-landed in the water in New York—the Miracle on the Hudson—crashed because it hit Canada geese. No wonder everybody is grumpy.

On the positive side, unwelcome houseguest or not, it's a still handsome animal, with that classic arched neck profile and a nicely balanced black, white, and gray color pattern. When not grazing lawns, they eat blueberries, waste corn, wild sedges, skunk cabbage: salad and more salad. The Canada goose (or, if you prefer, *Canadian*) comes in S, M, L, and XL. Size varies with subspecies; one of the smallest versions, the cackling goose, breeds in the Aleutians and has been split off as its own species.

Only one look-alike has to be considered: the small saltwater goose that passes through coastal California. Very black and white, it looks a bit like a Canada goose but is darker, more tidal. Called the brant, Humboldt Bay is a good place to look for it, but they're also in Morro Bay, Newport Bay, and even the Salton Sea. Low tide exposes eelgrass beds, a favorite food.

Meanwhile, most staycationing Canada geese show no inclination of returning to their migratory ways. Golf course owners unhappy with the freeloading geese have tried all kinds of tricks, from Mylar strips to sonic alarms. The best defense may be the cheapest— just hope some coyotes move into the neighborhood. The price is right, and as a solution, it's certified organic.

In making war with nature,
there was risk of loss in winning.
—John McPhee

Compared to the Canada geese (above), brant geese (right) are darker, more coastal.

Long neck, brown body, black beak and legs—must be a Canada goose.

Wood Duck · *Aix sponsa*

Some animals just seem too good to be true, and the male wood duck is one of them. The ladies make do with more modest speckled tan, set off with white cat-eye sunglasses. Males have the white stripes and red bills of a true dandy. With both sexes of wood duck, the name fits; while they always need to be by water, they nest in trees, and unlike other ducks, wood ducks have feet adapted for perching and climbing. Most often seen in parks or botanical gardens, historically they would have been best looked for in the gallery forest and oxbows of the Sacramento River, or perhaps above a beaver pond or deep in a flooded grove of cottonwoods.

Looking at these sharp birds it's nice to remember that humans can do things right, at least some of the time. Once declining to the point of extinction, now with better conservation and a supply of nest boxes (which they'll use as readily as their original tree cavities), the wood duck can presently be found across the US, including in the inland parks and nature reserves of California.

Wood ducks are normally seen in onesies and twosies, since they normally do not join up in large flocks.

Like other ducks, they keep themselves waterproof and tidy by using the tips of their bills to groom their feathers with oil. Their success at this gives us the expression *Like water off a duck's back.*

I am made to love the pond and the meadow,
  as the wind is made to ripple the water.
                    —Henry David Thoreau

Mutt Ducks, Park Ducks, and Muscovies

Most towns in California have city parks with a lake or pond, and in each lake there lurks, quacks, or waddles a bizarre duck-like animal that will not fit any category of bird you have ever seen before. You ask yourself, "What *is* that thing?"

Is it a mutant from an experiment gone awry? Are we downstream from a nuclear power plant?

Welcome to the world of mutt ducks, strays, and feral hybrids. Most started out as one of two things: the mallard (see the next page) or the Muscovy, a once-wild duck that in its native form lives in Mexico and South America and now loves city parks. Those two species have been domesticated for food and fancy, producing an array of colors and hairdos that can baffle experts. The pet ducks escape (or are released) and breed with other mixed-up mutts and natives until you end up with Prom Night in Zombieland. Mallards have successfully mated with over forty other duck and geese species: it has, shall we say, a great generosity of taste when it comes to dance partners.

If it is large and has red bumps on its face, it is some mix of Muscovy duck. If it has some version of the classic Daffy Duck bill, then no matter how white or pinto it is, how ponderous or petite its caboose, or how strange its mohawk, then it is indeed a mallard… or was once.

> *Rufus T. Firefly: Hey! Do you want to be a public nuisance?*
> *Chicolini: Sure! How much does the job pay?*
> —*The Marx Brothers*, Duck Soup

Top left started out as a Muscovy duck. The other three offer their spin on mallard genetics.

Mallard *Anas platyrhynchos*

 lakes, rivers, bays, city parks

World's most widespread duck—that could be one motto on its business card, or maybe *Green head, orange feet, what's not to love?* If you've eaten Peking duck, it started out as this species (maybe thousands of years ago), and almost any wetland, bay, pond, or city park that has wildfowl has some mallards as part of the selection. The term "robust population" applies here: American hunters shoot 4.5 million mallards a year (half a million in Arkansas alone), yet you won't notice any fewer when you go on your next walk. They're also hunted in California (including by falconers), and so far they show no overall decline here either. Maybe that is because they are very good at nesting, even in hedges behind swimming pools or along the backwaters of Disneyland. They also eat what's abundant (grass), supplementing that with worms, aquatic insects, shrimp, and any picnic handouts you're willing to lob their way.

The poet May Swenson says that a pair of mallards are "sunny baskets / [that] bear ripe light." Gal mallards stay a streaky, well-camouflaged brown, while the gents (except in a molt called eclipse plumage) sport the characteristic mallard pattern: yellow bill, green head, white necklace, brown chest, gray body, curly black tail feathers. Males are aggressive and want to mount any female they meet, and any implied similarity between ducks and human culture is entirely coincidental. As mentioned on the previous page, mallards around city parks and golf courses can display a rainbow of unexpected hues, including being all-white, and they are sometimes larger than the typical wild mallard. It's a bit like dogs: go to the pound and you will see how many variations there can be on the basic canine template.

To feed, the butt tips up, the head goes down, and grazing happens underwater. The *quack quack* so familiar to us all comes just from the female duck. Mallards are native across the Northern Hemisphere and are more or less present year-round in California, with some movement from the uplands to the lowlands in winter. A migrating duck can fly 55 miles an hour, a respectable speed and a useful thing if you're trying to get from central Canada down to northern Mexico. There are a lot of miles to cover—and a lot of waiting shotguns to dodge in Arkansas.

Color varies by sex, as illustrated by this classic male (left) and these two views of females (above).

A Californian's Guide to the Birds among Us : **21**

Northern Shoveler *Anas clypeata*

👀 lakes, rivers, bays, city parks

In fast-food restaurants, clerks are trained to upsell us—"Do you want to supersize that?" Here's a duck who said yes once too often, at least in the schnoz department. When it comes to beaks, northern shovelers can outdo any duck in the pond. You can almost hear them bragging. "You call that a bill? Now *this* is a bill!" The male's all-black bill looks like a cross between a garden trowel and the kind of power spade they use to crack open asphalt during street repairs. It is lined with one hundred small serrations, a bit like the baleen plate on a whale. They use those when filtering tiny shrimp and seeds out of the water.

Otherwise we have a basic duck-like duck: paddles in ponds, tips over to feed, flies far and well. Look for it both inland and in coastal lagoons, but not out to sea. Though mallards have green heads and some brown lower down, on shovelers the white patches are quite extensive (while never being more than a band on mallards), and all mallards have yellow, less shovel-like bills. Female shovelers can have pale bills and, like other female ducks, are mostly streaky brown; in all sexes, colors, phases, molts, and permutations, the elongated super-scooper bill finalizes their ID.

If there is a northern shoveler, should we also watch out for southern shovelers? Yes, but only near the bottom of the globe: Australia, South Africa, and Patagonia have three more shoveler species, and they won't be up here ever. We share our kind with the rest of the Northern Hemisphere, where it has the same shape and habits and color pattern. It occurs from Iceland to Iran and has new names in every country, but it's hard to top American vernacular. Former names for the shoveler were butter duck, cow frog (from its calls), spoon-billed teal, and swaddle-bill. Oh, for the good old days.

A shoveler looks like a mallard with a super-scooper bill.

Surf Scoter   *Melanitta perspicillata*

👓 sea, surf, sometimes bays

Cross a mallard with a puffin and you will have this orange-billed, black-bodied ocean duck. The name's long *o* rhymes with "registered voter" (and is not a typo for scooter). They breed on lakes in northern forests and tundra, and they winter abundantly off the California coast. Most years they arrive by November and move back north in April; biologists counting from headlands during spring migration have seen 10,000 a day moving north. Surf scoters are not limited to any one area of coast, and the species can be seen as easily from the shoreline at Malibu as it can during wave events at Mavericks. They also winter around the Channel Islands. A few nonbreeders say to heck with all that to-and-froing, and they stay put in California all summer long.

Males not only have the white-and-orange oversized bill, but the velvety black body and head received a lick of primer as an afterthought, showing white behind the neck and on the forehead. As is usual, females dial it down a bit: dark-billed and dark brown in general, their faces just show a smudgy patch of white. Hunters on the eastern seaboard call scoters "coots," but the two birds don't look or act much alike. Coots graze lawns while scoters are saltwater birds and eat by diving down to collect shellfish and other invertebrates, especially mussels. A good place to study scoters is from long piers.

Two other scoters join this one in smaller numbers: the black scoter (yellow bill) and white-winged scoter (white wing bars). Scoters can show up on inland reservoirs and aqueducts but that's super rare; almost all your sightings will be along the coast.

With this or any of our truly oceanic birds, including puffins and shearwaters, the question might be "What do they do in storms?" After all, even the coast guard has "no-fly" days. The answer basically is "ride it out": they do come into harbors and bays, but they never wait things out on shore—the name is accurate, as they are indeed very surf-adapted. Call it the kowabunga bird.

Look for scoters by breakwaters and in the surf—even the *big* surf.

Bufflehead *Bucephala albeola*

 lakes, rivers, aqueducts, bays

Buffleheads are among our smallest ducks and also the most clearly patterned. Saltwater or fresh, this winter visitor is equally common in bays, lakes, estuaries, and even the California Aqueduct, that ribbon of water and concrete connecting the Sacramento–San Joaquin Delta with the thirsty cities of Southern California. In all habitats it gives a little forward porpoise leap as it dives, stays under a few minutes, then bobs back up like an ultra-buoyant cork, sleek and dry. What is it doing under there? Eating plants usually, but also shrimp, crabs, and snails. In summers it goes north, nesting in woodpecker holes in Alaska and Canada.

The head pattern is bold, especially on the males. To some it looks like a shield from medieval heraldry, or else a child's version of a cop car. The name comes from "buffalo head," after the prairie grazer whose dense, broad head this duck's noggin resembles. "Princess White-Wing" is one way to translate its Japanese name, and indeed the bufflehead does have a broad white V on each wing, clearly visible in its low, skimming-the-water flight. Female and immature buffleheads have a smaller amount of white on their heads than males; winter flocks can show a mix of head patterns but usually include at least one classic male to help clinch ID.

One duck in particular can be confused with this one. Hooded mergansers look similar but have oval heads and more stretched-out, chopstick-shaped bills; brown, compact bodies; and a preference for smaller ponds and quieter backwaters. They're usually found in ones and twos, and are scarcer overall. Lucky times, if you find one: to realize your bufflehead is actually a hooded merganser is to reach into your pocket for a dime and come out with a silver dollar.

Be like a duck. Calm on the surface, but always paddling like the dickens underneath.
—Michael Caine

Unlike a bufflehead (right and bottom right), the hooded merganser (below) has a straight, very thin bill.

Ruddy Duck   *Oxyura jamaicensis*

👀 lakes, rivers, city parks

This duck is called ruddy for the color, not ruddy in the sense of an irate Englishman saying "get that ruddy duck off my lawn." The body is a deep, saturated chestnut, a color made all the more cock-a-doodle-doo by the male's bright blue bill and immaculate white cheek blaze. Summer or winter, the compact size and upswept back tail (often cocked at a jaunty angle) help us learn this from the other ducks in the lake. Duller, browner females have a dark cap and a stripe under the eye that goes from the edge of the bill back to the ear. This breaks up the profile when it's sitting quietly on the nest, and females carry the same basic look all year long.

Ruddy ducks dive to feed, catching insects and larvae, often at night, which leaves them free to nap and look cool during the day. Expect them in the bottom half of the state in summer and statewide in winter. We would like nature to be a Peaceable Kingdom, but in the breeding season ruddy ducks can bully each other fiercely—and are bullied in turn by coots. Somebody hand out the T-shirts that say *Can't we all just get along?*

Inland summer marshes have a small, equally chestnut duck, the cinnamon teal, but it is all one color, never white-cheeked and stiff-tailed, and is more elongated, with a black bill that calls to mind a scaled-down shoveler's bill.

We're used to complaining about the European starling and the equally European house sparrow, but in the UK they curse an introduced population of ruddy ducks, which mess with rare local ducks and take over parks. From Britain it has spread to mainland Europe—as has the Canada goose—and our native bird is now their park pest.

In winter (left), ruddy ducks have plain bills and brown (not chestnut) bodies. Summer (below) brings a blue bill.

California Quail *Callipepla californica*

It doesn't matter what California means; what does matter is that with all the names bestowed upon this place, "California" has seemed right to those who have seen it. And the meaningless word "California" has completely routed all the "New Albions" and "Carolinas" from the scene.
—John Steinbeck

Like some kind of sandwich-boarded ad man shilling for the Windy City, the California quail calls out *chi-CA-go chi-CA-go* over and over. If you're from the San Fernando Valley, you might hear "Pacoima, Pacoima," or if you're an avid museumgoer, "Picasso, Picasso." A quail covey on an outing—potbellied dad in front, a scurry of little ones trotting along behind—looks cute to us, and probably like coupon day at KFC to a hungry hawk or coyote.

Males bust out every color pattern possible: black face and white stripe; chestnut and white on the top of the head; gray, tan, and chestnut on the chest and belly; brown wings, and a scramble of scales and white teardrops in between. A blobby feather juts forward from the top of the quail's head as if it's wearing a Renaissance cap in a school play.

Quail count as upland game birds in hunting regulations, though there seem to be enough to go around: this is a very widespread bird, most common in chaparral and oak woodlands, yet also ranging into suburbia. Expect it statewide except for on the highest slopes of the Sierra Nevada.

In the lowland deserts the Gambel's quail replaces it; it looks similar to the main California quail but has a tan chest and a black lower belly. It really wants to sell some real estate, so it adds a spin to the call: *chi-ca-go-go*. A more elusive quail of pine forests, the mountain quail has top feathers that stick up like two thin, wavy, Martian antennae, and white-and-chestnut zebra stripes running up and down along the sides. Hiking firebreaks at dawn is a good way to find this one.

Ring-necked Pheasant *Phasianus colchicus*

👓 fields, marshy uplands

First brought to California as a game bird, pheasants are colorful, long-tailed marshland and open field mega-chickens. They split the difference between our native quail, all of which are smaller, and introduced turkeys, which are larger, plainer, more likely be found in oak woodlands, and more likely to be seen in a gang, rafter, or flock (pick the word you like best).

Look for pheasants along roadsides in rural California or in the larger wildlife refuges north of Sacramento. You might see it just foraging like a quail along the side of the road, or bursting from cover to take a short but vivid flight. "Vivid" is perhaps too quiet a word, since male pheasants blaze with more color than a Thanksgiving ad for Target. Where should we start? There's the iridescent green head with bright red bare skin around the eyes, the bold white neckband, the cinnamon underparts with black spots, the fancy tail, the yellow bill. Even the females are a golden buff, densely vermiculated with black bands and spots. No wonder every hunting catalog in the country puts it on their cover at least twice a year.

In some ways this is an Eisenhower-era bird. Used to be if you liked the outdoors, you showed that with a leaping trout or strutting pheasant decal on the back of your camper shell. And back when farming was small-scale, non-corporate, and a bit approximate, and back when water was sloshed around freely, California had a lot of pheasants, all of them thriving in hedgerows and unmowed pastures and barley fields from Stockton to Redding.

That has changed. One of the indicators is a 90 percent decline in the number of pheasants taken by hunters on public land. Should we care? Probably, yes, since pheasants are not only attractive in themselves but also indicate other changes in the environment. Thinking about the status of the pheasant may well lead us to think about lots of other beings too, from shrews to beetles to loggerhead shrikes, and perhaps a species we like even better than those, namely ours.

Dawn rises over South San Francisco Bay.

California Marshes, Then and Now

Instead of the Golden State, California could have been the Tule Marsh State. From Redding in the north and all the way down to the Grapevine, the Central Valley was once an immense network of marshes, lakes, and rivers. Until livestock production caught up with the population growth, gold rush forty-niners were fed turtle soup for the first year. The turtles were hauled out of Central Valley lakes and marshes by the tens of thousands. The wetlands were later diked and drained and turned into almond orchards, walnut groves, and tidy rows of cotton and lettuce.

Coastal estuaries had associated marshes too, as did parts of the Owens Valley and the Klamath Basin. Salinas was first named Crane Lake because of the thousands of sandhill cranes found there. In flood years, the entire Central Valley turned into a continuous lake.

Altered, lessened, managed, and yet still defiant, California's wetlands keep coming back, like the prizefighter who just won't quit. Cattails line drainage canals and storm basins; city parks and golf courses attract red-winged blackbirds and tree swallows. From the Mojave Desert and a freshwater marsh called Piute Ponds, to the Klamath and Tule Lake wildlife refuges in Siskiyou County, birdwatchers can still look for marshland specialties in dozens of prime locations.

Finding beauty in a broken world is creating beauty in the world we find.
—Terry Tempest Williams

A white-faced ibis catches breakfast at Piute Ponds in Antelope Valley.

Pied-billed Grebe · *Podilymbus podiceps*

 lakes, rivers, ponds

Now you see it, now you don't: a pied-billed grebe (small as a bathtub's rubber ducky) can be swimming along, obvious as anything, and when you glance away and look back, it's gone. They can submerge with a stealth that bests the navy's top submarines, either doing a quick forward dive or just blowing the ballast valves and sinking silently from view.

Shorter-necked and stubbier-billed than western and Clark's grebes, pied-billed grebes can be found on reservoirs and large lakes but also make use of smaller ponds and stiller backwaters. Those other two grebes will even go out to sea, but the pied-billed grebe is a lake and pond specialist, rarely staying under more than a minute or two, and apparently making a good living off the smallest minnows in the pond. It takes tadpoles and craw-dads as well. Under the water, it covers long distances. It sinks down in one place only to reappear surprisingly far away; if you kayak over there or jog along the bank for a better view, down it goes, slipping away again.

Another small grebe, the eared grebe, might look like this species, but they're the ones that form rafts on Mono Lake; you won't see pied-billed grebes in huge flocks. Instead, the dabchick—to use the utterly perfect folk name—prefers cattails along the edges of ponds, and is more often found in ones and twos. The young have great black swirls like marbled pound cake, but brown adults just get the one black circle on the pint-sized bill, and sometimes a fluffy white butt for accent. They nest in reeds, and adults give the little chicks piggyback rides, really tempting one to use anthropomorphic words like "cute." Anybody remember the 2003 remake of *The Italian Job*? This small pond bird is the Mini Cooper of the aquatic world.

Typical adult postures (below and top right). Young ones have swirled stripes on their faces (bottom right).

Western Grebe and Clark's Grebe

Aechmophorus occidentalis and *Aechmophorus clarkii*

It's hard to know what to do with grebes. They're not quite ducks, not quite loons, and even the name is odd, with few linguistic associations. Play it in Scrabble, most of your opponents will just shrug. Yet California has six native grebe species (plus a seventh, out-of-range stray), and this pair, western and Clark's, can be found statewide and year-round in lakes, estuaries, bays, and the surf zone of the ocean.

All grebes dive for fish, their lobed feet propelling them like torpedoes underwater. To tell western from Clark's, study the face. Both are elegantly and cleanly black above, white below, but on Clark's, there's more white between the eye and the beak, and the bill is more strongly orange. Western grebes have a yellowy green bill and a dark patch between eye and beak. Otherwise they're twins, and mingle in mixed flocks in winter.

Both western and Clark's grebes enact elaborate courtship dances, and both nest on the water, constructing mini islands of floating vegetation. On their expedition, Meriwether Lewis and William Clark did discover new birds (the Clark's nutcracker, for instance), but this one is named for a different nineteenth-century naturalist. Unlike eastern and western meadowlarks, the "western" part of "western grebe" is not to distinguish it from an eastern form (there isn't one) but just to indicate that its home range is the American West, as it is found not just in California but from Seattle to the Dakotas.

Clark's grebe (bottom) and western grebe (left). Loons (right) look similar but have heavier bodies, thicker necks, and stouter bills.

Rock Pigeon   *Columba livia*

cities, towns, exurbia's edges

Which domesticated animal produces the most show breeds? Maybe it's dogs, or what about horses—pinto, palomino, Shetland pony, Budweiser Clydesdale. No, it's the sky rat or rock dove or park pigeon, which in its fancy, domesticated forms (blue tumblers and crested picards, rollers and tippers and pouters) fills the world with over a thousand different breeds. If you sit in a city park tallying all the moochers shouldering each other out for popcorn or birdseed, you might spy ten or twelve kinds just in one flock.

Native to North Africa and/or Western China, the pigeon has been a city bird for 5,000 years. The Romans ate pigeons, as did Americans into the 1940s. (It was called squab.) Poet May Swenson says she loves "the rainy greens and / oily purples of their necks." And despite the variety of possible colors, most feral pigeons do default to the basic pattern: red eyes, shimmery green or purple head, gray body, two dark wing bars, and coarse red feet. More times than not there's a tiny white saddle draped across the base of the beak. Plump and low-slung, they walk with a head-bobbing gait and plenty of muttered tut-tutting and low, liquid coos. They can also grunt, and when they take off, their wing tips slap together like a small burst of half-hearted applause.

Darwin kept and bred pigeons; as carrier pigeons they served the US Army in two world wars; today, they provide a pesticide-free food source for skyscraper-nesting peregrine falcons. Pigeons also remind us how many weeds and wads of grass survive in our vacant lots and roadside edges; they mostly eat seeds, and those seeds have to come from somewhere (besides human handouts). True, nests become solid masses of fossilized crud over many years, and if you're trying to clean that out, be sure to wear a mask. A gang of pigeons roosting over your car or patio is not a pleasant thing. But the pigeon has been in North America almost as long as the Puritans have, and they manage to live and thrive in almost every

city in the world. It's hard not to admire that, and hard as well not to imagine that, after the zombie apocalypse, pigeons will still be here even when we are not.

Eurasian Collared-Dove *Streptopelia decaocto*

 cities and towns, including desert outposts

Smaller than a pigeon, bigger than a mourning dove, collared-doves can be found in every city in California—and in every town, farm, ranch, village, trailer park, homestead, military base, hippie commune, and desolate two-outhouses-and-a-Quonset-hut outpost. On the way to Death Valley you can find them in Darwin, population 35, but they also nest on Santa Cruz Island, and in Beverly Hills and La Jolla, and Oakland and Eureka and Sacramento and Redding. Poke your head out the front door—if it's daylight, you can probably see one in your yard right now.

The ones here in North America started as cage birds in the Bahamas. In the 1970s they escaped, colonizing Florida by the 1980s. Fifty miles one year, one hundred the next, the range expanded, and a map documenting their spread radiates in concentric circles like the shock waves of an earthquake or nuclear explosion. It's not unexpected; this pattern echoes their spread in Europe. Native to Asia, they moved into Europe in the nineteenth and twentieth centuries. In North America, they occur in every state, Arkansas to Alaska, Maine to Arizona, and so the collared-dove is (it seems) now here to stay.

Pinky tan with dark wing tips, in all but the youngest stages it shows a diagnostic black half-collar where the neck meets the shoulder; mourning doves never have that. Both coo, but mourning doves have longer, more pointed tails and a slimmer profile, whereas collared-dove tails are broader and end in a clean, squared-off tip. Pigeons are usually much darker overall and chunkier, and, unlike mourning doves, they never show a long, visible-in-flight "bridal train" tail.

For a hundred years Los Angeles had spotted doves: an Asian species, it looked like a mourning dove but with a large black patch on the back of the neck, spangled with white dots. In the early 2000s, they almost all disappeared mysteriously. What happened? Nobody knows. Collared-doves don't seem to have had anything to do with it, and they also don't seem to impact mourning doves. Could it be that we have a non-native species that—like the palm tree or European honeybee—causes no harm? If so, give them a nod for carrying out the least militarized invasion in history.

In the mountains, band-tailed pigeons reverse the pattern: white band, dark neck.

Mourning Dove *Zenaida macroura*

👀 fields, towns, deserts, woodlands

North America's most common native pigeon (and perhaps most common native bird period), the mourning dove, can be found everywhere in lowland California. It certainly does well in cities, but it also occurs along streams and wood edges, in the deserts, on ranches and farms, and in the Sierra from the foothills to the lower pine forests. Small-headed and long-tailed, mourning doves have a scattering of black teardrops on the wings, with pink legs and a dinky beak. Overall, the body is—well, what? Are they a pinky gray? A tannish buffy beige? We don't do well describing the "you can't see me, I'm planet-colored" range of hues. The tail has white tips with a bit of black. If you want to see your first one, watch power lines in any leafy suburb.

Some groups of animals have special herd names. For this species the collective noun is "a pitying of doves." And true, there is a mournful aspect to them. It's not the squeaky whinny (created by the shape of its wing feathers) when they take off, but when they are *whoo-cooing* so slowly and with such a plaintive longing, it does indeed sound sad. *Coo-OOO-whooo.*

A ground bird when feeding, the mourning dove eats seeds almost exclusively and is both abundant and abundantly shot at by America's hunters: the national take per year may top 20 million doves. (Fewer die in California, of course, where hunting declines yearly—we would rather go snowboarding, or invent a new kind of electric car.) What's surprising is not that it flourishes even when hunted, but how well it has done despite the arrival of collared-doves in California. They can easily be told apart: the collared-dove has a black hindneck. The arrival of a robust competitor seemingly has not lessened the mourning dove's population—at least not yet.

The beginning of wisdom is to call things by their proper name.
—Confucius

Greater Roadrunner   *Geococcyx californianus*

👀 deserts, chaparral, brushy grassland

A classic icon of the Southwest, the roadrunner is a robust, ground-running cuckoo with a long beak, long tail, shaggy crest, and blue face patch. Both sexes look the same (streaky black, brown, and white), and it is a pretty big bird, averaging about two feet long. Snakes and lizards and more snakes and more lizards are what it chases down and eats, supplemented with small birds and mice or, at a trailer park once, a daily dish of ground hamburger on a blue ceramic plate. No other color would do: it had to be the blue plate. When swallowing horned lizards (known to some as horny toads), roadrunners need to be sure to get the poor beast oriented the right way so they don't choke on the spines.

If we had to pick the most characteristic, clichéd, expected roadrunner habitat it would be scrubby desert, from downtown Palm Springs to the Colorado River, but this is also a chaparral and grassland bird, following the western Sierra foothills almost to Oregon. You might see one run across the freeway on-ramp one morning, or catch a glimpse of its short, gliding flight between patches of ceanothus.

If you're hiking, roadrunner tracks are easy to identify because two toes point forward, two back, creating an X pattern. As a general note, more birds leave tracks than you might guess, from quail to herons, and studying the trail ahead may also let you see (and not walk on, and thus not erase) raccoon tracks, coyote tracks, or even the saucer-round paw prints of a mountain lion. When people say that hiking is good cardiovascular training, does that include how hard your heart pounds when you realize you missed a puma by just a few minutes?

*The Hopi believe the roadrunner
protects against evil.*
—Jane Miller

Juniper and sandstone—the perfect place for lizards and the roadrunners that eat them.

White-throated Swift *Aeronautes saxatalis*

cliffs, mountains, freeway overpasses

Marcel Proust said, "Beware of dangerously simplified generalizations," but this is one case where it's fair to say that all swifts (everywhere in the world) are just that, *swift*. The word and the object match exactly. Swifts are very good at flying but not useful at all on land: their weak feet can't do much more than cling to the side of a cliff long enough to make a grass-and-spit nest. They even make love midair, with two, three, or four birds pinwheeling downward in a mass of black and white, only to break apart just before the ground as each one zooms off and climbs back up to open air. Sometimes they misjudge and hit the leaves of the forest floor. If you ever have felt woozy after romance, you can sympathize.

The genus name means "air swimmer." These cliff-nesters launch like targets from a skeet-shooter's catapult, flying straight into the air without hesitation. Coming home is trickier, yet they can aim for a thin slice in the cliff and hit the target exactly, folding their wings at the last moment to zoom inside. When not on the nest, they'll roost communally in a slit crack in the cliff face, and it's not just one but many in a row that aim, tuck, and disappear like magic.

A bird of the American West, in summer they can be found from Yellowstone to the Grand Canyon. Look for them hawking insects around cliffs, above mountain lakes, and even in downtown L.A., since they have learned to nest in the drainage holes in freeway overpasses and other urban infrastructure. In winter some migrate to the Amazon, but along the Central and Southern California coasts, many stick around all year long, active on all but the coldest days, when they may wait for warmer weather in a mild torpor.

Swifts nest in cliffs, mountains, and freeway overpasses.

Anna's Hummingbird *Calypte anna*

👀 gardens, city parks, streams, chaparral

The eastern US has only one species of hummingbird (ruby-throated), while California has a dozen. Of those, this is the most widespread, centering its range on California but going as far north as Alaska and south into northern Baja. It mostly lives west of the Sierra but has outposts as far east as Las Vegas and Reno. Females and immatures are green above and grayish-whitish below—nice enough, one supposes, but to catch a flash of the male's magenta head and throat in bright sunlight is to experience a micro supernova of flaming pink.

The voice is bright and *zsseety,* and ranges from a monosyllabic *ztik* all the way to a full cantata. Displaying males rise high, higher, highest, then plunge straight down, with an explosive *pop*—created by air snapping through tail feathers—as the brave pilot pulls up just before hitting the deck. Females watch from perches in the shrubbery, as indifferent as most girls are when boys rev hot rods and peel rubber.

Both male and female Anna's hummingbirds can be found in an encyclopedia of habitats: towns and suburbs, chaparral and deserts, streams and hilltops, meadowlands and pine forests. As settlement changed California's botany, hummingbirds benefited. (See also the entry for Allen's hummingbirds.) Anna's hummingbirds start nesting as early as December, seemingly too early for spring flowers. Yet suburban yards offer feeders and exotic plantings, while in parks and along median strips, eucalyptus flowers are a winter treat.

The "Anna" of Anna's hummingbird has a pedigree longer than the bird itself. The bird was named in the nineteenth century in honor of Anna Masséna, the Princess d'Essling and Duchess of Rivoli, who was the wife of the son of one of Napoleon's marshals. That's more history than we need: if you know anybody named Anna, just say it was named after her.

> *The answer must be, I think, that beauty and grace are performed whether or not we will or sense them. The least we can do is try to be there.*
> —*Annie Dillard*

Four views of Anna's hummingbird (left) show its range of color.

The black-chinned hummingbird (above) has a purple and black (not magenta) throat.

Allen's Hummingbird *Selasphorus sasin*

👓 coastal slope gardens and parks

California's other backyard hummingbird (see also Anna's hummingbird) has more color in the body than Anna's does, as the males blend green and cinnamon throughout, with a small yet intense red throat patch. As with other hummingbirds, that gorget can look black unless the light catches it just so, and then presto, the color bursts out in full iridescent glory.

Allen's hummingbirds live here year-round, except when they don't—some stay put and some migrate to Mexico. Their calendar feels a bit accelerated, since northward migration happens as early as Christmas, and they're on their way south again by late May. Their range expands yearly as they adapt to our lush and quasi-tropical backyard plantings. Once strictly coastal (and more southerly), Allen's now follows the fog belt north into Oregon; in Southern California, it has filled out the urban basin from Palos Verdes inland to Hemet.

All hummingbirds run their engines at high rev, so they need a lot of high-octane fuel. Famously, a hummingbird can eat twice its body weight every day, and yes, they can fly backward. Nests are made from spiderwebs and lichen. The smallest bird in the world is the bee hummingbird of Cuba, one of about 320 species of hummingbirds, all confined to the New World—none are native to Africa or Asia, where the larger, slower sunbirds fill this niche.

The Aztec god of war was a hummingbird, and they can be fiercely territorial around feeders. One solution? Plant more flowers in your yard and put out more feeders. When there's enough to go around, nature once more enters Pax Romana.

No such thing, the queen said, as too many sequins.—Mark Doty

Birdwatching Inside the Museum: The Role of Specimens

The US has a strong tradition of preserving books and archives for the common good, visible in everything from small-town libraries to the miles of books in the Library of Congress. Less well known are the state's outstanding collections of natural history specimens. Often located in the back rooms of museums, rows and rows of drawers and cabinets contain the voucher specimens that document size, color, location, DNA, and even stomach contents. Archived items can range from passenger pigeon eggs to tiger pelts to a drawer of pink flamingos.

North and south host equally fine resources. Berkeley's Museum of Vertebrate Zoology houses a collection of over 185,000 bird specimens (the largest in the state), while San Francisco's California Academy of Sciences adds another 96,000 specimens. The Natural History Museum in Los Angeles preserves 120,000 bird specimens, and the Western Foundation of Vertebrate Zoology holds a world-renowned egg collection. These repositories are libraries not of books but of natural history itself.

The deceased birds enter into collections many ways. Some come from zoos, others get donated by hunters, and still others have flown into windows or been hit by cars. Ornithology was and still is a shotgun science, based on the premise that "if it's hit it's history and if it's missed it's mystery." (The painter Barnett Newman had that relationship in mind when he said that art history is to painting as ornithology is to birds.)

Citizen science helps as well; to contribute your own range and date records, see Appendix II for details about the eBird database.

Throbbing with attitude, this Anna's hummingbird (right) is clearly saying, "You talkin' to *me?*" Digital records now supplement (but do not replace) physical specimens.

Kimball Garrett examines an Anna's hummingbird specimen from 1917.

A tiger skull in its archival box, ready to be reshelved after study.

American Coot   *Fulica americana*

👀 lakes, ponds, bays, city parks, golf courses

This is the black "duck" (not a true duck, just looks like one) we know from every lake and park. Coots live year-round and statewide in marshes and still water, from the coast up to the lower pine forests, but rarely at high altitude and never in swift water. To feed, they tip their butts up, grazing on plants underwater, or submerge fully if the pond is deep or enemies loom overhead. They also feed on land, and early gardeners struggled to get the lawns established in Golden Gate Park since the new grass attracted so many coots.

Graceful they ain't—coots take a long time running along the water trying to reach flight speed, and on land the waddling gait makes them look like they're all wearing Baby Huey diapers. In the water this poor duffer does better, and the lobed feet are perfectly engineered: broad on the downstroke but folding neatly on the upstroke. Look at them closely next time you see this bird browsing on shore; even a lie-flat colander from a trendy kitchen store can't beat the design.

Sticking to its own or comingled with other waterbirds, coots cluster in flocks, especially in winter. There is no flashy seasonal variation—always the same charcoal gray body, stubby white beak, short neck, plump body. They are vocal and territorial, more so in breeding season, and will chase even large ducks aggressively. Night or day you can tell coots from ducks by their strange style of swimming, since the head bobs forward as if tugging the body behind it like a toy cart on a string: head-body, head-body. Studying in good light lets one appreciate the way water beads on their backs (like flecks of oil bouncing off a superheated pan) or notice the seemingly malevolent red eyes. What thoughts are they thinking in there? Nothing bad against us, we hope.

True affluence is not needing anything.—Gary Snyder

Black-necked Stilt *Himantopus mexicanus*

 marshes, estuaries, rivers

Daddy longlegs, longshanks, marsh poodle, yelper—American folk names for the stilt are all pretty good, but none top the bird's name in Spanish: *candelero,* "the candlestick bird." Tall, boldly colored, and irritatingly loquacious, stilts join avocets in being the easiest two shorebirds to see and name. Unlike the summer/winter alternating wardrobes of avocets, stilts pick one set of formal wear and hold to it year-round. And unlike most other shorebirds, which swing up to the Arctic to nest in twenty-four-hour-a-day sunshine, stilts breed closer at hand. They can be found all year in San Diego (especially on old saltworks), L.A. (the Los Angeles River among other places, such as at the Willow Street crossing), and in South San Francisco Bay (saltworks again). A few usually make it to Arcata and inland reservoirs, and also to the Owens Valley, but the real lollapalooza for stilts is the Salton Sea, with many thousands breeding, loafing, feeding, and yapping continuously.

On average, stilts stick to shallower water than avocets, but the preference is only slight. Thin, straight bills help stilts nab a variety of water-edge prey, including caddis fly larvae, brine flies, tadpoles, beetles, snails, and a small quantity of plant seeds.

Watching a stilt work its way along a salty shoreline, one question often comes up. The stilt has very long, noticeably red legs. Why do their knees bend backward compared with ours? The answer is that like many other animals, a stilt walks on its toes, so that what is our ankle is actually their knee, and the joint that matches our knees is tucked up higher into the body. (You can see that joint if you watch them fold their legs to sit down on open ground.) We start with the same pieces of paper as stilts do—we just fold our origami differently.

American Avocet *Recurvirostra americana*

 marshes, estuaries, rivers

Dipping their heads low, avocets sweep shallow water back and forth, back and forth, as if groping after lost car keys. They are checking for invertebrates and don't care if the water is fresh, brackish, or salt so long as there's a good mix of muck and murk. They often pair up with black-necked stilts or a range of other, smaller shorebirds, but in any crowd, avocets will be the tallest, slimmest shorebird present.

Pale blue legs last year-round, but head color changes by season: summer gives them a cheerful cinnamon-colored head and neck, while the winter side of the avocet wardrobe is foggier, more sober: just a muted gray. Both versions have white bodies and black-and-white wings. Sexual dimorphism means variation in the sexes, the way a male African lion has a mane or a rooster has a fancy tail. In avocets it's less obvious: both males and females feed by walking along, head down, and both also search for food while swimming, but where you see the difference is in their upswept bills. On males it is straighter and longer, while females have shorter, more curved bills. In both, alarm calls are a repeated *kleet kleet,* a bit like somebody squeezing a pet's chew toy over and over.

Some animals excite human imaginations more than others. John James Audubon had a charming avocet painting, and if you follow the market for folk art, you may have noticed the abundance of avocets in amateur wood carving. The combination of slim elegance and bold summer colors apparently proves irresistible to some craftspeople, even attracting those with remarkably little aptitude. If it looks good on the mantel, perhaps that's all that matters.

Head color in winter (top left) and summer (right). When the birds are in molt (above), you can see a mix of head colors in the same flock.

Black Oystercatcher *Haematopus bachmani*

👀 tide pools, breakwaters

This one is easy to see but hard to know well. Strictly coastal, black oystercatchers like tide pools and breakwaters (the first clue for identification), and they look the same in all ages: slightly chubby black (or dark brown) body, with chalky pink legs and a vivid red bill. Up close, an orange eye ringed with red accents the plain face and gives your camera's autofocus something to lock on to. From Alaska to Baja, this guy is a West Coast specialty, even viewable from the car along the shoreline roads of Monterey.

Contrary to the name, they don't eat many oysters, and nobody "catches" an oyster anyway. Hammering, prying, jabbing, pulling—if your specialty is rocky shore shellfish, you've got to work hard. The question is not "Why live by tide pools, crowded with yummy limpets and mussels and crabs and barnacles?" but "How are you going to get these hard-shelled, glued-to-the-rock littoral animals off of the substrate and pried open for eating?" One trick is to find a partially opened mussel under the water, jab a beak in, and cut the abductor muscles (the part that can slam the two shells tight shut). Foraging skills may be a mix of innate predilections and learned-from-mom tricks of the trade.

This bird is easy to spot but hard to follow for very long. Nervy and active, it flies point to point, often disappearing out of view around the crashing-wave side of the rocks, leaving us slipping and sliding behind, wondering where everybody went.

While you're watching black oystercatchers, keep an eye out for the smaller, more mottled sandpiper. Black turnstones also forage in the same crashing-wave, slippery-rock tide pools as oystercatchers. Half the size of an oystercatcher, the black turnstone has orange legs, a white belly, a mottled black back, and a dark, fairly abbreviated bill. Turn-

stone flocks chatter and rattle with contact calls, seemingly ignoring you—that is, until you try to scramble closer for a picture.

Point Pinos in Pacific Grove is a good place to see your first oystercatcher.

Killdeer   *Charadrius vociferus*

👓 fields, marshes, rivers, city parks

Heard as often as seen, this robin-sized plover is one of the few shorebirds you don't need fancy binoculars or a detailed cheat sheet to identify. That's partly because of its color pattern (the two chest bands and cinnamon rump tell all) and partly because of its cocky make-a-go-of-it-anywhere attitude. Unlike most other shorebirds, you can discover killdeers in overgrown parking lots, in the middle of soccer fields, along the edges of storm drains and aqueducts, by the cement berms of sewage ponds, in marshes and wetlands, at golf courses, or even in the most sublime and picturesque of subalpine meadows.

In all habitats, killdeers feed and nest on open ground, and while on patrol will sprint forward, pause, hold still a moment, and then spike a beak to snag an insect or the pink end of a worm. The nest is the most minimal of scrapes. Both the male and female lure humans and stray dogs away from eggs and young with either a broken-wing display or a puffed-chest bluff charge.

Even the name is easy to remember, since it mirrors the scolding call: *kill-deeer kill-deeer*, most often heard as the bird circles overhead, vexed at your presence.

Walking, I recite the hard
explosive names of birds:
egret, killdeer, bittern, tern.
—Robert Hass

Double chest bands (below and right) help confirm ID.

Semipalmated plovers (above) look like baby killdeer except they are smaller than killdeer and have only one black chest band.

Long-billed Curlew Numenius americanus

 beaches, estuaries, inland fields (rarely)

In an overhyped, oversold, overheated world, thank goodness for honesty. Here is a case of getting exactly what's promised. Does it say *curlew, curlew*? Check. Does it have a long bill? Double check. And in fact, "long" seems too paltry a word. A nine-inch bill on a three-inch head looks almost as if the beast got stuck in a candy store's taffy puller. On a person, that would be like walking around with a pool cue lashed to your face. In the curlew's case, let the drilling begin: no matter how deep the worm or crab or shrimp tries to burrow, this curlew can dig down after it. (They also can nab insects from the grass or beach.)

As with sister species in the worldwide curlew group, the American kind is a big shorebird with a duck-sized body, a wingspan of thirty inches, a stonking huge bill, and a set of plumage colors that have been scribbled in with all the tans and browns in the pencil box. It breeds in central prairies and joins us in winter, hunting on tidal mudflats and also inland in pastures, muddy lakes, wet meadows, and flooded fields. To rest, it turns its head around 180 degrees so its bill fits along the curve of its back, disappearing from sight like a sword sliding into a scabbard. How do two long-billed curlews celebrate their honeymoon? Very carefully.

A second beachgoer could trick you into thinking you've run into a curlew, though maybe one only half-grown or that got shrunk in the wash. The whimbrel has the same color of body and it too has a long bill, but on whimbrels the bill is more reasonably proportioned, and a whimbrel has a sharper black-and-white stripe pattern on the head. Both were hunted for meat in the nineteenth century and both are protected today.

Whimbrels (below) have shorter bills and bolder crown stripes than curlews (bottom).

Marbled Godwit *Limosa fedoa*

🔭 beaches, estuaries, coastal wetlands

A fairly large shorebird (as marsh birds go), the godwit has a pale pink or orange bill that is curved up, not down, and a body that is not one solid color but instead offers a swirling blend of brown, black, and tan. A meadow breeder in the Dakotas and Canada, it's usually gone from California by late spring but is already back again by midsummer, and some nonbreeders stay year-round. Marshes, beaches, tidal flats, and coastal wetlands are its usual digs, with migration shipping it to unexpected places, including golf courses and desert sewage ponds.

Female godwits are larger than males, allowing them to feed in deeper water as the tide comes in. To confirm species ID, check the beak. Curlews and other shorebirds have shorter or downward-curving bills. Only the avocet has a similar bill that is long and swept a bit up; unlike godwits, though, avocets are always white-bodied with a gray or cinnamon head, and they feed by sweeping their heads from side to side, while godwits lance and probe.

What does the name mean? Dictionaries claim "origin obscure," though "wit" echoes birdcalls generally, and we like two-syllable nouns: a shorebird called a lapwing is also called the peewit, and a dull person is a dimwit. In the UK, traditional names for godwit have included yardkeep, half whaup, scammel (a term that appears in Shakespeare), pick, prine, and jadreka snipe.

As a culture, we seem to have fewer names for birds than we used to, now replaced by a surplus of words for soda pop, kinds of guns, and people of any race not our own. If you know any poets, take them birdwatching with you. Perhaps they can help reverse this trend.

In Newport Bay, godwits rest with mixed sandpipers and dunlin.

Why Do Shorebirds Have So Many Different Bills?

Few groups of birds have bills as varied as the shorebirds. From godwits to curlews to killdeer, they have evolved more tools than a Swiss Army knife. These bills—long or short, turned up or curved down—cover every possible option for probing, prying, digging, plucking, stabbing, and snatching.

Experts call this "resource partition." The idea is that, in a given mudflat, the worms and crabs and clams burrow to different depths, so no single tool is ideal. By specializing, each species will have the best tool for one circumstance and thus will be the best at that job, while an adjacent species will be better equipped to deal with food that is deeper, fatter, thicker-shelled, or just more elusive. It's like the nursery rhyme that claims "Jack Sprat could eat no fat; his wife could eat no lean"—the same beach offers something for everybody.

We live in a good place for experiencing this phenomenon. The official California bird list explodes with a total of sixty-eight shorebirds, including plovers, phalaropes, oystercatchers, one native snipe and two from Europe, and lots of little guys called peeps or stints. You're unlikely ever to become bored looking at stilts and avocets, but if you do, the other shorebird species will be waiting for you in all their chittering, restless, confusing plentitude.

From top to bottom: Killdeer (short, stout bill—plain but utilitarian); least sandpiper (midsized bill on a very small bird); whimbrel (medium-long bill, curved at the end); marbled godwit (long, thin, upswept bill, dark at the tip).

Sanderling *Calidris alba*

 beaches

You know this sparrow-sized bird by sight if not by name: it's the pale beach sandpiper scampering along the wet tideline, always in a hurry. What would be the best group noun—a hurry of sanderlings? A scurry of them? Like Monty Python's knight who won't surrender, it just barely misses getting wiped out by one wave and then races back to the edge to dare the next breaker, only to be chased back up the berm again. Black legs and a black bill help us separate it from a few other generic sandpipers (like the western and least), as does the white comma curled at the shoulder. Up and down the beach, just on the very edge of disaster, the sanderling outruns the waves on a blur of frantic feet.

The sanderling lives in California in winter, but that winter stretches generously from July, through Christmas, and all the way to May, when the sanderling hurls its hundred-gram body into the sky for the long trip north. It migrates to the tundra, breeds, and flies back home a few months later. (How much is a hundred grams? Less than a hundred paperclips.)

If you're small enough and quick enough, beaches make good buffets. Picking, grabbing, and probing as it runs, the sanderling hopes for fish eggs, flies, mole crabs, marine worms—anything that is small, juicy, and wiggly. Sometimes a monster wave crashes down and in unison the flock lifts up, circles, and sets down a few hundred yards farther along.

Usually sticking higher up on the dry, high-tide part of the beach, the snowy plover looks as pale gray as the sanderling but chases waves less actively and always has a stubby, bushtit-like bill. No Alaska for this little guy: it nests right on the beach—or tries to. The easiest way to see a snowy plover is to look for roped-off sections of sand with a sign: *Caution: Snowy Plover Nesting Area.* On weekends or on the Fourth of July, snowy plovers probably wish they had come up with a different life plan.

Pixar's charming film *Piper* is based on this species.

Willet *Tringa semipalmata*

beaches, estuaries, tide pools

In families, middle children often complain about being invisible: the older kid gets all the firsts; the youngest is spoiled as the baby forever; the middle child just gets hand-me-downs and that tired *Oh, not you too* voice. The willet, too, is a middle child. Plain gray and middle-sized, it is not the fastest or the smallest or the longest-billed or the most migratory. It is not the loudest or the most surprising in any way—at least not until it flies. Then, the black-and-white wings unfurl like a medieval battle flag and suddenly it seems as if the English will win the Battle of Agincourt after all.

Early Puritans, new to this species and praising modesty, named them "humilities," since willets only show their finest colors to God. The genus name translates as "mirror bearer," another reference to the snazzy wings. A biologist might label the wing panel less a psalm of praise and more an alarm signal, since the sudden flash confuses predators and alerts flock-mates. The common name transcribes the call, though more than one beach-stalking photographer has sworn the name comes from the shooter's muttered fretting of "Will it fly? Will it fly?" Just as you get close enough for a killer shot, off it goes.

In summer this species is a prairie nester; a few willets don't even leave the state, nesting from the north end of the Owens Valley on up into the big lakes of the northeast. Winter beaches find willets mixed in with curlews, godwits, and sanderlings. Willets walk deliberately at water's edge, watching the bubbling air holes reveal burrowing crabs or mollusks just as the waves recede. From Laguna Beach to Half Moon Bay, you almost certainly have seen this species before, even if you didn't notice. Pity the middle child, overlooked yet again.

A poem can be as much about forgetting as it is about remembering.
                                        —Mark Yakich

Tufted Puffin *Fratercula cirrhata*

👀 rocky offshore islands, open ocean

Many people dream of taking an Alaskan cruise, but in the case of puffins, some Alaskan wildlife is willing to come to us. The southern-most breeding colony of tufted puffins in the world is on a pile of granite less than thirty miles from the Golden Gate Bridge: the famous Farallon Islands. On a clear day—yes, they do happen—you can see San Francisco from the Farallones, which also have seal colonies, breeding gulls and cormorants, and a few hardy biologists counting sharks and mist-netting lost warblers. You can't land on the islands, but birdwatching trips go out by boat to look for puffins and seabirds, and as the happy (if seasick) passengers will verify, to see a puffin in the wild, its white head and massive orange bill glowing intensely in fog or sunlight, is one of wildlife watching's true high points.

Puffins nest in burrows dug into the cliff face. They bogart these holes from other seabirds or can dig them on their own. It may be that at least a few of the gold rush forty-niners ate puffin-egg omelets. With food for the settlers at a premium, eggers rowed out from the mainland to fill gunnysacks with murre eggs and anything else they could grab; puffins could have been among the by-catch. This was a period of brutal, heartless exploitation, and it's estimated that a million eggs a year were hauled off the islands. That lasted until 1881, when some protection was finally instituted—and by then, chicken ranching would have been cheaper anyway.

The tufts in the bird's name refer to thin streamers flowing backward like the ponytail of an aging rock star. Set off against a white face, these look quite lovely. In midwinter the puffin is drabber but still has an orange bill, and the summer finery returns in mid-March and lasts into fall. Puffins can be seen from shore once in a long, long while (and will be cited on birders' message boards if so), but the usual encounter happens on a boat trip.

Keep some room in your heart for the unimaginable.
—Mary Oliver

Heermann's Gull *Larus heermanni*

 beaches, bays, out to sea (rare inland)

We expect seagulls to be white-bodied and gray-backed, and then we have this contrarian, who reverses that pattern by going with an all-gray body set off by a blazingly white head. This is usually a beach-and-ocean bird, rarely found inland. In spring, most Heermann's gulls breed on islands in the Sea of Cortez, dispersing to mainland Mexico and the California coast the rest of the time. As gulls go, it's smaller and quicker than most; in a brief flyby at sea it might be mistaken for a sooty shearwater, but notice the broader, shorter wings and the orange or red bill.

Like all gulls they'll mooch trash or find their own fish, but Heermann's gulls also stick close to brown pelicans, hoping that a few stray anchovies will escape from those big pouches and flop their way. Because 90 percent of the world's population nests on just one island, there's concern that two or three El Niño years in a row (when warm water sends food elsewhere), or even one mega-hurricane, could really do serious harm. On the sly, more than one biologist has sent out telepathic suggestions urging Heermann's gulls to colonize Alcatraz or Catalina or some other safe haven, just as a genetic insurance policy.

Adolphus Heermann was a nineteenth-century naturalist. He surveyed transcontinental rail routes and invented the word "oology" (the study of eggs). Urban legend has it that he died from syphilis of the brain, but the immediate cause was a self-inflicted gunshot wound when he stumbled and fell on his rifle. If you want to wrap up a Heermann twofer, his other namesake, a kangaroo rat, can be found on the Carrizo Plain.

There is a curious idea among unscientific men that in scientific writing there is a common plateau of perfectionism. Nothing could be more untrue. The reports of biologists are the measure, not of the science, but of the men themselves.—John Steinbeck

A first-year bird (right) shows a brown body and a two-tone bill.

Ring-billed Gull *Larus delawarensis*

👀 beaches, harbors, lakes, city parks

Roger Tory Peterson, the great artist and inventor of the modern field guide, owned 10,000 slides of the ring-billed gull. He was no more obsessed with it than he was with any other species, but they lived on the beach near his home, and any time he bought a new camera lens, he walked down there to try it out. Ring-billed gulls became his go-to test subject.

Smaller than California and western gulls, the ring-billed gull has a paler back than both of those kinds, and its bill is slimmer and the black stripe on the bill more cleanly delineated. (The California gull can have a blotchy black band on the end of its bill in some age cycles, creating possible confusion, but it's never the clean black rubber band of a ring-billed gull.) Like California gulls and unlike pink-legged westerns, ring-billed gulls have yellow legs.

The ring-billed gull is a buoyant flyer. They can hover adroitly and pluck tidbits out of a boat's wake or the surge of an incoming tide. Unlike the more pelagic western gulls, ring-billeds stick to beaches and harbors, rarely going out at sea. They also forage inland, scrounging at dumps in winter (and returning at night to the beach to roost), while in summer they migrate over the Sierra to nest at Mono Lake and prairie states farther north.

Along the coast, ring-billed gull numbers really pick up in winter—that's the time to study all of our gulls, especially if you are willing to follow each sentence by saying, "Well, it *may* be this one, but who can really tell?"

Form is a template to be modified.—Mark Yakich

Western Gull   *Larus occidentalis*

 beaches, estuaries, city parks, out to sea

This is a big, bossy gull, ready to claim the best picnic leftovers and equally willing to land on the back of a dead whale far out at sea, perhaps staying with the putrid carcass for weeks. They used to be ocean birds mostly, nesting offshore and not going inland, but landfills and city parks have lured them deep into town, sometimes fifty miles from the ocean.

Our largest common seagull, western gull adults are bulkier, darker-backed than others, and all-white below, with pink feet and a red dot on the bill. (This is the target nestlings peck at to trigger feeding.) The youngest ones are mottled gray-brown, and that shifts into mixed white and gray until the final adult pattern resolves itself. Any given flock will have a dozen mix-'n'-match combinations, but a few clean, unambiguous adults always help sort out ID. There are fewer gulls on the beach in summer when they disperse to offshore islands. Studying western gulls there, biologists have to wear hard hats or else nesting gulls would peck holes in their heads. As is, the gulls dive with such force they can knock grown men over.

The sound of a seagull is exactly like…the sound of a seagull. Is it a sort of *screoww screoww*? A *scree scree*? Hear it in a sound track and you instantly know you're at a quaint fishing village or in the middle of a pirate movie. At the Salton Sea, similar gulls have yellow legs and feet and are called yellow-footed gulls; once thought to be the same as western gulls, they are more closely related to birds in South America. Along the coast, species like glaucous-winged gulls and herring gulls can hybridize with this one and create a maddening blur of color phases and options. At Monterey's Fisherman's Wharf, gulls will pose for point-blank pictures, and sooner or later a western gull will give you a classic pose, and that *chik* sound will be another species checkmarking itself onto your list of certified sightings.

*Kelp closes up
where the bird has just been.
—Emily Wilson*

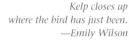

These birds have all reached full adult plumage.

California Gull *Larus californicus*

👀 beaches, bays, parks, inland lakes, out to sea

To ID a gull, look at the shape of the bill, the color of the back, the color of the legs, and the overall heft and posture. Compared to other gulls, the California gull is a Toyota Camry sort of seabird: midsized and dependable, never flashy or overstated. The bill is straight and mid-length; the back is a middle shade of gray; the overall body is midway between the largest gulls and the smallest ones; the legs are a regular kind of yellow; the migration route is not the Arctic to the Antarctic and back again as some terns manage, nor yet is this gull a stay-in-one-place-all-year kind of refusnik. They may fly five hundred or one thousand miles, but they come back soon enough. In winter, look for them in all the usual gull places: beaches and harbors, landfills and playgrounds, fields and reservoirs, tide pools and kelp beds. By early summer many have headed inland to breed, but they are usually back before school starts in September, ready to pick up where they left off.

Ironically, the California gull is the state bird of Utah. Its service to the Beehive State came during the initial Mormon settlement, when it saved crops by gobbling up an invasion of insects. Today it is also remembered as the bird that helped save Mono Lake. Tens of thousands of California gulls nested there, but lowering lake levels—a result of insatiable Los Angeles overdrawing the water supplies—were threatening the entire gull population. A significant legal victory by the Save the Mono Lake Committee now requires the lake to be maintained at a healthy (or at least less catastrophic) level.

In other places, the California gull's success raises a different question. Recently, the birds have been breeding in the salt pans of South San Francisco Bay. There were twenty-four nests in 1980; the site grew and grew, and it's up to 45,000 gulls today. That is a lot of mouths to feed, and since they eat baby terns and other neighbors, it's starting to become a worry. When do we cull one species in order to protect the others?

That's a dangerous topic to raise, given where humans might be placed in that list.

A subadult (center) with second winter plumage. Mono Lake (bottom right).

How to Age Gulls

In Shakespeare's time to gull somebody was to trick them, hence the word "gullible." Now the gulls do the tricking, since they can be head-scratchingly hard to tell apart. Figuring out how old a gull is can help reliable identification. California has two-year, three-year, and four-year gulls. The numbers refer to the time each group takes to go from just-out-of-the-nest juvenile plumage to full adult regalia. To become good at gull ID—a strange hobby, but compelling to some—one starts with age (the bird's, not yours) and season (winter or summer).

Below are four winter plumage cycles for the western gull. You can find this seagull on just about every beach from San Diego to Oregon, and it's a good one to study first, since most other gulls have similar sequences. Things to review include the bill color, the amount of "clean" gray (versus blotchiness) the back shows, and how much all-white the head has begun to show.

Out of a big winter flock of thousands of gulls, a few may show plumage worn pale by abrasion (from blowing sand), a few may be hybrids (a blend of more than one species), a few may be birds usually found to the north or east, and some can look odd if flat light or some other trick of circumstance distorts perception. Yet even so, despite these occasional obstacles, most groups of coastal gulls should have some individuals that closely match this series.

A gull, up close, looks surprisingly stuffed. —John Updike

Left, from top to bottom: western gulls in first-year, third-year, and fourth-year (adult) winter plumage.

Above: Second-winter western gull.

Elegant Tern *Thalasseus elegans*

🔭 beaches, bays, estuaries, coastal waters

The usual birder's joke is that elegant terns are truly elegant…until they open their mouths. They go *kraa-eek kraa-eek,* loudly and gratingly and incessantly, until even the most patient person wants to say, "Oh, come on, guys, give it a rest." Most California terns are smaller than gulls, longer-winged, and coastal, with long, often yellow or red bills and a zippy flight style punctuated by plunging dives. They are after small fish—anchovies in particular, or any of the minnow-sized, surface-schooling things that fishermen call bait fish.

You might see these hovering over yachts in a marina or resting on a breakwater, sometimes intermixing with gulls. On a protected beach or sandbar, elegant terns are the midsized ones. Smaller terns include the least tern (dinky, with a yellow, black-tipped bill) or they might be side by side with the largest tern on the beach, the Caspian, which has a substantial red bill and nearly gull-sized body. Terns on the beach have shorter legs than gulls, and they always have longer, more lance-like bills.

Like Heermann's gulls, most of the elegant terns in the world nest on islands in the Gulf of California, and like black skimmers, they are recent colonizers of San Diego and Orange Counties. After nesting they disperse north up the coast, and from July through late fall can be expected in Monterey, Half Moon Bay, Bodega Bay, and all the way up to British Columbia. El Niño years make them more common than usual in the northern half of the state, but they always stick to the coast; this is hardly ever an inland species. Winter sends them the other way, along the entire Pacific coast of South America, from Panama to Chile.

> *We are here on the planet only once, and might as well get a feel for the place.*
> *—Annie Dillard*

An elegant tern seems small compared to the Caspian terns on either side (bottom left).

Black Skimmer   *Rynchops niger*

This is a bird that looks put together from spare parts. That bill? Just impossible. The lower part sticks out past the top part, and the whole thing is way too long for the rest of the body. The legs are seriously stubby, and the folded wings jut too far out the back end. Only when put into action does the whole package come together: a swift, buoyant, water-skimming flight style, a knife-sharp bill that shears the water like scissors cutting silk, and lighting-quick reactions that let the bill snap shut the instant it touches a fish. Like other terns, skimmers are beach nesters (including the beaches formed by spoil islands), and they need calm, shallow water to forage. Other than that they don't even need daylight: skimmers can fish at dawn and dusk or even in the middle of the night.

The black skimmer is a recent arrival. Usually one thinks of it as a Texas or East Coast bird, with a subtropical range extending to South America. Yet birds are rarely static. Starting in the 1960s, the black skimmer sidled from Texas to Baja, and by the 1970s it had made the shift from there to the Salton Sea and San Diego, then to Bolsa Chica in Orange County, and then in the 1990s up to Santa Barbara. From there it carried on even farther, and now it nests around the margins of San Francisco Bay.

How did they know where to find the next piece of open habitat? They didn't know, not exactly. In a mechanism called post-breeding dispersal, some species wander during late summer, and skimmers that have been banded at the Salton Sea have ended up as far away as Arizona and New Mexico. Sometimes exploring new territory doesn't work out (the New Mexico bird finally died), but through this vagrancy and dispersal a population might accidentally discover a great place to start a new colony. After the San Francisco Bay colony, could they end up breeding in Oregon? It seems unlikely, but then again every part of this bird is unlikely in the first place, so it just might work out.

Sooty Shearwater *Ardenna griseus*

👓 open ocean (sometimes seen from shore)

Pismo Beach, Hearst Castle, the Piedras Blancas lighthouse—in August along the Cambria coastline, two rivers run parallel. The inland river shimmers with tens of thousands of cars bumper-to-bumper on Highway 1, all packed with bored teens and grumpy dads, everybody chasing the perfect vacation. Meanwhile, there is another river just offshore, this one a continuous stream of sooty shearwaters migrating back to New Zealand. Some days they're so close you don't even need binoculars.

These wind-riding seabirds follow the surfer ideal of endless summer. Their slim wings and cigar-sleek bodies mean they can cross the ocean with enviable freedom, "shearing" the water to get free lift and glide off the surface of waves. Their calendar traces a 40,000-mile-long figure eight. From breeding cliffs in New Zealand, they cross the Pacific to the Gulf of Alaska, then swing south to Monterey Bay, where half a million birds molt, rest, and eat. As they diagonal back home in late summer, they run the length of the California central coast before heading back out across the Pacific.

Shearwaters eat krill, the same half-inch-long shrimp that whales like, and also squid and small fish. Food availability varies, depending on upwelling (where currents bring cold, nutrient-rich water to the surface). If you miss seeing these birds from the elephant seal lookout near San Simeon, just take a Monterey Bay whale-watching trip any day from July to October. Where you find the humpbacks and blue whales, you'll almost always find sooty shearwaters. Sometimes they are so full of krill they can't even fly.

Birders in Southern California know this bird as well, but from shore in the south you are more likely to see a black-and-white kind called the black-vented shearwater. Try looking for them from Point Vicente or La Jolla Cove. In winter, these are good cliffs for watching gray whales, too.

In Monterey Bay, going to see whales often means finding shearwaters too.

Double-crested Cormorant   *Phalacrocorax auritus*

👀 rivers, lakes, reservoirs, rocky coastline

All cormorants are big, black, snake-necked ducks that have a Loch Ness Monster profile when swimming. Seen on shore drying their wings, they look like scarecrows holding open wet shirts. They all have long beaks and chase fish underwater. This species can be found in the ocean or in fresh water, where it usually prefers lakes and reservoirs. You would expect it in the L.A. River, for example, but not in Yosemite or at Mono Lake. Flocks of cormorants fly in a line like geese; one way to ID this species is by looking at the neck in flight. Two other cormorants live in California (both only by the ocean), but of the three, the double-crested cormorant flies with its neck coiled back in an S. The other two, the pelagic cormorant and the Brandt's cormorant, fly with the head and neck stretched out straight. They look like a row of chubby black arrows.

The stretched-arm pose on shore makes for dramatic (and Christlike) photos but is just to dry out wet feathers. With less oil waterproofing their plumage than other waterbirds, all cormorants have to be mindful of getting soaked, and so spend part of their day warming up and drying out. They will do this while perched on power lines, ship masts, trees, or just rocks by the shoreline. If you have binoculars, this gives you a chance to study the vivid yellow-orange throat pouch and the intensely emerald (some say aquamarine) eye.

There are forty cormorant species worldwide, including the flightless Galapagos cormorant. An alternate name for members of the group is "shags"; *Austin Powers* jokes aside, "shag" and "cormorant" mean the same thing, just like the words "heron" and "egret." When you have a chance to get up close to a double-crested cormorant, be sure

to check out the eye, and try to decide if it's turquoise, aquamarine, emerald, or just blue. Whatever term you vote for, it's shagadelic, baby.

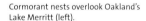

Cormorant nests overlook Oakland's Lake Merritt (left).

American White Pelican *Pelecanus erythrorhynchos*

👀 inland lakes, ocean bays sometimes

White pelicans are inland birds, with an added interest in bays and coastal lagoons in winter. They are bigger than brown pelicans and often travel longer distances—as the dark wing tips reveal, since black pigment beefs up durability. In our region they nest in northeastern California and at Pyramid Lake north of Reno, wintering at the Salton Sea and other inland bodies of water. In migration they can be seen more or less anywhere, even over Yosemite Valley. One radio-tagged white pelican crossed the Sierra fourteen times in one year. Topaz, Mono, and Crowley Lakes are good places to watch for migrants in the eastern Sierra, and a great pleasure (and great surprise) is spotting a flock of white pelicans paralleling Highway 395, the line of white birds contrasting with the skyline of the Sierra escarpment.

All white pelicans are surface scoopers, sometimes working cooperatively to herd their prey into the shallows. Their elastic pouched bills hold up to three gallons at a time. This capacity makes human fishermen envious and at times suspicious. Are they eating up all the fish? Probably not: most of that is just water, and in the course of a day, white pelicans don't eat that much overall for such a big animal.

Like a panting dog, hot pelicans in summer flutter their throat pouches to increase airflow across their blood vessels. Young birds are dingier, but adults are always bright white, sometimes with a badge of yellow on the chest and a small swoosh of horn on the top of the beak. Pelicans don't walk well and may need a long running start to get up into the air, but once flying, their migration paths can cross continents.

Migrating pelicans stand out against eastern Sierra scenery (top right). Breeding birds (lower right) show more yellow and have knobs on their bills.

Brown Pelican *Pelecanus occidentalis*

coastal ocean, bays, the Salton Sea

Except at the Salton Sea, brown pelicans stick to the ocean, leaving freshwater lakes to their larger, all-white cousins. They are found everywhere along the California coastline, as well as along the coasts of Baja, the Gulf of Mexico, the Atlantic, and down into Central and South America. While they have been spotted as far as one hundred miles out to sea, usually they stay closer to land, diving from thirty, forty, fifty feet up to catch anchovies, sardines, and mullet (the fish, not the haircut). Air sacs beneath their skin help absorb the impact, and even when they submerge fully, they shoot back up and start flying again, almost as if the whole thing never happened. Gulls and terns chase after them, hoping to snatch anything that spills out.

There's some minor color variation, with younger birds just plain brown all over and older birds having pale heads and, in breeding condition, red throats. Not so long ago brown pelicans were endangered because DDT had been wrecking their eggs. Populations are now recovering, with birds in California breeding on offshore islands, and this population growth is supplemented by birds moving north from Mexico. They're big enough not to have predators but they put themselves at risk around humans fishing from piers. Some pelicans have learned to become shameless beggars, and not only is this undignified and unhealthy, but being around so many fishing poles means they're in danger of getting their pouches snagged on fish hooks.

Native Americans both ate pelican meat and used their feathered skins in ceremonies, in some cases making pelican cloaks with abalone buttons. The bones were turned into whistles. Pelicans still feature in popular culture: Geoffrey Rush was a pelican in *Finding Nemo*. There are no pelicans at Pelican Bay, a supermax prison near the Oregon border, but most people remember that Alcatraz Island in the San Francisco Bay is named after an archaic Spanish word for pelican, a word adapted (and mistranslated) from Arabic. In modern Spanish, "pelican" now is just *pelícano*.

Brown pelicans have a wingspan of six to eight feet, and a line of them silhouetted in flight adds a great foreground subject for pictures of red sunsets—ready, aim, tweet.

Great Blue Heron *Ardea herodias*

👀 lakes, rivers, parks, rocky coastline, wet fields, meadows

So long as you're not a fish, bullfrog, or gopher, it's hard to think of anything bad to say about this majestic, easily studied bird. In flight it seems unhurried, even stately, cruising like a monarch surveying her realm. Along a pond edge or in the middle of a pasture, the great blue heron has the patience of a Zen master, staying present in the moment for hours, waiting for a chance—just like *that!*—to lance out its neck and grab the intended prey. That beak really gets the job done: there is a story about an irate great blue heron that nailed a pinewood oar so hard the bill stuck out two inches on the other side.

Their nesting colonies (called heronries) are in the tops of tall trees and often include great egrets, black-crowned night-herons, or double-crested cormorants. They'll use cotton-woods in the Sacramento Delta, eucalyptus trees in San Diego, or the who-knows-what-they-were dead snags still standing in the Salton Sea. To hunt, great blue herons are equally unfussy. Find them in parks and by lakes, harbors, storm drains, irrigation canals, fish hatcheries, and even offshore, balanced on mats of floating kelp. With a six-foot wingspan and a look-you-in-the-eye standing height, you might think it's heavy as a small person. Yet hollow bones and other efficiencies help the whole package weigh just six amazing pounds.

This bird can turn up in the least expected of locations, like in the top of a Joshua tree. (That's a pretty good sign there's a marsh or golf course nearby.) It also exemplifies convergent evolution: the great blue heron is found all over California and North America, while in Europe the same role gets filled by a species called the grey heron, and Africa has a supersized version called the goliath heron. Science fiction writers used to imagine the canals of Mars filled with water. If that ever comes true, we can bet that the Martian version of the great blue heron will be there waiting for us.

Egrets and herons are not cranes, which have a different lineage. Two sandhill cranes (above) are alert for prey.

Great Egret   *Ardea alba*

👀 lakes, rivers, parks, rocky coastline, wet fields, meadows

Raise high the roof beam, carpenters—another grand and tall bird coming through! The great egret is the stunningly white bird seen in wetlands and parks throughout the California lowlands. It is nearly the same size as (and very closely related to) the great blue heron. Not just a local species, it has worldwide distribution.

Why so successful? Among many other things, the great egret eats frogs, voles, snakes, fish, crawdads, mole crickets, muskrat kits, and even birds called black rails—and everything larger, smaller, and in between. (Rails are ultra-secretive reed dwellers whose ability to melt into the marsh gives us the expression "thin as a rail." Great egrets catch them during winter tides, when rising water pushes rails into the open.) Hunting methods include all the usual heron/egret tricks, from stalking, waiting, and gleaning, to jumping and hopping to stir up water, to quick marching and lots of twisting, peering, dipping, and jabbing.

One hundred years ago there were almost no great egrets left in California, since they were the victims a worldwide fashion cataclysm that killed millions and millions of nesting birds. At its most intense, the demand for feathers in the millinery trade made prize aigrettes (as the fanciest feathers were called) worth twice as much as gold. (As Werner Sombart said, "Fashion is capitalism's favorite child.") The Audubon Society helped save the birds (see page 66).

I don't ask for the sights in front of me to change, only the depth of my seeing.
—Mary Oliver

Snowy Egret *Egretta thula*

....

👓 lakes, rivers, parks, rocky coastline, small ponds

Snowy egrets do everything that great egrets do, but more quietly, more modestly, and in even more out-of-the-way places. They're fine patrolling breakwaters or canals or the shores of big lakes, but they'll also investigate overlooked ditches and back bays, storm drain outfalls, and forgotten triangles of marshland. Like the great egret, they were hit badly by the trade in feathers in the nineteenth century, and like the other herons, they are still rebuilding their populations.

Telling this species from the great egret means judging size but also looking at bills and feet. Great egrets and snowy egrets are equally white, but the smaller snowy egret has a black bill (sometimes with a yellow base), while great egrets have a hefty all-yellow bill. Great egrets and snowy egrets both have black legs, but snowy egrets have yellow toes. They seem to use those as a distraction to rile up fish or perhaps startle them or even herd them. Maybe they just have yellow feet because it looks nice in the morning light.

About the same size as a snowy egret, the similar cattle egret has a yellow bill, thicker neck, and usually some yellow on its stockier body. It is originally a savannah species and should really be called a zebra egret or rhino egret after the big game it follows, snatching insects stirred up by passing hooves. In the nineteenth century, storms carried cattle egrets from Africa to Brazil, and once they were established there, they spread north through the Americas. Look for cattle egrets in fields and pastures, often with livestock.

Snowy egrets are smaller than great egrets and have yellow feet.

Black-crowned Night-Heron *Nycticorax nycticorax*

 marshes, reedy lakes, rivers, city parks

This is the one that didn't get the memo. We expect herons and egrets to be long-legged, long-necked, and graceful. (As the saying goes, *You can never be too rich or too thin*.) We also appreciate that rather than requiring dawn starts, most herons and egrets are willing to stand in plain view right in the middle of the day. Yet this species contradicts all that. For one thing, it is positively squat, or at least one has to call it "husky" or "well-built." As the name implies, it's also nocturnal, coming out at dusk, hunting all night, and then dropping back into the reeds at sunrise. And while it is a classic wait-and-stab predator, sometimes it even paddles around the open part of the lake like a thick-necked duck. What's up with all that?

Night-herons break the rules, but, in doing so, have found a very successful lifestyle. They live worldwide, and in California they can be found in park lakes, along coastal estuaries, in lowland marshes, and even ranging up to 10,200 feet. Immatures are streaky brown, while the gray-and-black adults look the same year-round, except in breeding season, when a few stray head plumes stick out like a decoration on a flapper's tiara.

They can also hunt during the day (and the other herons can hunt at night), but their main pattern involves clocking in for the night shift. Food includes frogs, tadpoles, and baby birds, but usually just fish, especially all things minnow-sized. Like other herons, they jab their target with a spear-thrust of the head, flip it around to orient it slippery-side first, then swallow it whole.

By day look for it resting in reeds or snoozing high in lakeside trees, the head pulled deep into the shoulders like somebody waiting for a bus in a rainstorm. At dusk you can see it silhouetted against evening light, flying across the marsh to find a good hunting perch. One folk name is "quork-shite," after its hoarse, squawking call. In a moment of linguistic echo, its scientific name is a tautonym, meaning the Latin repeats twice and so translates as "night crow night crow."

I often think that the night is more alive and more richly colored than the day.
—*Vincent van Gogh*

Adult (far left) and juveniles (left and below).

White-faced Ibis *Plegadis chihi*

....

👓 marshes, wet fields, rice farms, rivers (sometimes)

Greeny bronze and heron-sized, the ibis says, "By my bill you shall know me." Don't worry about the "white-faced" part of the name, which just describes a pale squiggle near the eye. Instead it's the overall shape that matters: long legs, dark watermelon body, long neck, and that long, gracefully curved bill. Nothing in the marsh is like it, not unless there's an out-of-range glossy ibis mixed into the same flock. (One ibis species lives in the west, one in the east, and even experts can barely tell them apart. If a nonconformist strays into the other's territory and is spotted, all the listers pogo dance with glee.)

In the 1960s and 1970s this bird was headed down the tubes, at least in California, but the population has now recovered, and thousands of ibis have returned to our fields and skies. Sometimes you'll see an ibis or two even in the city, such as along the lower L.A. River in Long Beach or over Golden Gate Park, but usually it's a species of wetlands and flooded fields, and so occurs at the south end of the Salton Sea and along the entire length of the Central Valley, from the Oregon border to Bakersfield. Inland Empire reserves, such as the San Jacinto Wildlife Area near Hemet, have ibis flocks, which in turn means that you may see a skein of ibis, long legs behind them, beaks leading the way, crossing above Interstate 15. You even can come across them in the desert, in and around the Piute Ponds wetlands east of Los Angeles.

This is not the same ibis species worshipped (and mummified) by the Egyptians, but perhaps it should have been. If the light catches the feathers just right, it is an intoxicating shimmer of bronze, purple, green, and gold, all layered over a maroon base coat. That you can see one from your car while driving home from work or doing the tour loop at one of the Sacramento wildlife refuges seems like a gift too unexpected to ignore. Maybe leave out some snails or a small frog as a sacrificial offering, or at least close your eyes and say "thank you" three times.

Ibis can be found even along the Los Angeles River in Long Beach.

Egrets, Herons, and the Feather Trade

Egrets and herons nest in colonies called heronries. In the nineteenth century hunters almost emptied these completely, shooting birds to get breeding plumes to use in hats. Besides herons, other types were harvested just as freely, including seabirds, warblers, jays, swallows, terns, and flycatchers. It seemed as if every species in the marsh would go extinct. Thanks to the Audubon Society and the UK's Royal Society for the Protection of Birds, nesting sites were protected and laws enforced. If you like looking at egrets and herons today, thank the spirit of your great-grandmother. She and women like her took off their hats and picked up their pens, writing the letters that created world-changing legislation.

The Audubon Society was named after but not founded by John James Audubon. A contemporary of Daniel Boone (and briefly in business with George Keats, émigré brother of poet John Keats), Audubon was America's greatest bird artist. His multivolume, large-format *Birds of America* was sold by subscription; most copies are now in museums and libraries, or else have been broken up into pages to be sold one by one. A still-intact copy recently sold for $10 million at auction. Audubon's plates brilliantly combine narrative drama, ornithological accuracy, and elegant design, the last of which was especially necessary since each bird was

portrayed full scale, even the flamingo, wild turkey, and whooping crane.

Lecturing once in Edinburgh on the correct preparation and display of bird specimens, Audubon had a particularly attentive student in the audience: the young Charles Darwin.

One of the great dreams of man must be to find some place between the extremes of nature and civilization where it is possible to live without regret.—Barry Lopez

Plumes flying, two ladies swirl through the Gilded Age (left). A snowy egret (below) reminds us that one bird was killed for just a few feathers.

Turkey Vulture *Cathartes aura*

👀 fields, woodlands, mountains, deserts

The turkey vulture may seem half-finished because of the naked head and its rocking, slightly inebriated flight style, but as Margaret Atwood asks, "Well, heart, out of all this carnage, could you do better?" Like other vultures, smell guides them unerringly to carrion. They will take a dead fish or random lizard, but as we all remember, vultures mostly circle over dead and dying animals, whether that is in Far Side cartoons or over the roadkilled skunk on the side of the mountain road. (Supposedly they know not to eat the scent glands.)

Flying and gaining altitude take energy; rather than spend that energy, vultures may stay in a roost tree until late in the morning, waiting for the sun to generate enough lift for them to ride thermals to cruising altitude, and then soaring with more glide than flap the rest of the day. Flight style helps separate them from hawks and eagles: turkey vultures hold their wings in a shallow V and often rock slightly side to side. Seen closer, the wings underneath are two-tone: the body and crossbeam form an all-black T, while the rest of the wing is paler, almost silver. Seen even closer, the red head becomes visible, and closer still, you can make out the yellow tip of the bill—though by that point you may need to check your pulse and be sure it's not you the bird is searching for.

In the American South they have black vultures, which are common in villages in the tropics as well; they have a black, not red, naked head and a different wing shape. In the Trojan horse department, an Arizona raptor called the zone-tailed hawk mimics the turkey vulture even down to its exact flight style, and thus camouflaged it can grab unsuspecting sparrows and squirrels. They'll probably never know what hit them.

> *Let us praise the noble turkey vulture: No one envies him; he harms nobody;*
> *and he contemplates our little world from a most serene and noble height.*
> *—Edward Abbey*

California Condor · *Gymnogyps californianus*

👀 Pinnacles National Park, Big Sur, Tejon Ranch

Doubters and haters take note: sometimes humans get it right. In the 1980s, with this species on a greased slide to extinction, the final twenty-two free-flying condors were captured, taken to zoos, and told to make whoopee as if their lives depended on it.

Fast-forward to now and we have four hundred condors, some still in captivity, but others establishing populations near Pinnacles National Park, along Big Sur, in Baja, in the Grand Canyon, and a few even turning up over I-5 by Six Flags Magic Mountain near Los Angeles or cavorting with hang gliders above the 210 freeway. With a nine-foot wingspan, the condor is one of the few birds that can glance at a hang glider and think, "Yeah, I could have a piece of that."

From the Ice Age until the nineteenth century, condors ranged across America, from the Channel Islands to New York. Lewis and Clark found them in the Pacific Northwest and John Muir watched them in Pasadena. What caused their decline? Besides habitat loss and poaching and turn-of-the-century egg collectors, they flew into power lines, got poisoned by lead shot, ate strychnine-laced bait set out to kill coyotes and bears, drank radiator fluid, lost chicks to golden eagles, and sometimes were just plain iffy about being parental.

ID is straightforward: naked head, huge wings, slowly gliding circles, and way more white in the wing than any other vulture or eagle. Plastic wing tags help researchers track who's gone where; they are coded three ways: by color, by number, and by dots or underlines beneath the numbers. If you see one, make a note and it might be possible to look up its name. Supplemental feeding has helped wild (or sorta kinda wild) condors become reestablished, with field crews often relying on the carcasses of stillborn calves donated by dairy farms.

Odd but true: to cool off, condors and vultures pee on their own legs, letting evaporation do the rest. Will it work for humans? Try it and see.

Osprey   *Pandion haliaetus*

👀 rivers, lakes, bays, coastline

A big black-and-white fish-snatching hawk with bent wings, that's the osprey—with *long* bent wings, if seen well. The black bandit's mask paints a thick line from beak through eye and ties behind, leaving white the top of the head and the neck, chest, and undercarriage—another color combination that helps certify identification. Always over or near water, it builds a big stick nest on poles and tall trees, and hunts over lakes, reservoirs, bays, and rivers, including the very urban and channelized L.A. and San Gabriel Rivers.

Ospreys catch a fish by diving headfirst toward the water, swinging up in a power skid at the last minute to extend the feet (talons ready), making the hit, and powering back up into the air again with a mighty whoosh of six-foot wings, the captive prey shocked and wiggling in the grip of talons. The scales on an osprey's feet have small barbs to help keep a good grip. Should we spare a thought for the poor fish that was swimming along and minding its own business one minute, then finds itself one hundred feet up in the air the next? It's also interesting to watch how an osprey turns a fish lengthwise in its talons for better aerodynamics.

In the rest of the U.S.A. ospreys are summer birds, going to Mexico and South America to fish away the winter, but they are year-round in the Orange Belt states of California and Florida, their numbers greatest during fall and spring migrations, when they even can be found far out in the desert. Where the range of ospreys overlaps with bald eagles, the eagles will harry them until the osprey drops its fish, which biologists call "kleptoparasitism" and the eagles just call being at the top of the food chain.

Life is cruel? Compared to what?
—Edward Abbey

An osprey nests on a tufa mound at Mono Lake (bottom right).

Bald Eagle *Haliaeetus leucocephalus*

👀 lakes, rivers, reservoirs, rocky coastline

Big, sexy, iconic: you know it instantly, and even a child can tell you they're not really bald. Here are things you probably don't know about bald eagles: they are monogamous and mate for life; among birds of prey, only the condor has a bigger wingspan; a better name would be white-headed fishing eagle; they were affected by DDT but are recovering; they now nest near cities (but didn't used to); waterlogged while hunting, if they get downed in a lake they can row to shore; they can gather in winter roosts of hundreds of birds; out-of-range bald eagles have turned up in Bermuda and Sweden. And for a footnote that covers both eagles and waterbirds, coots can get locked in place in lake ice by rare but ultra-sudden freezes. In Big Bear, locals call the ice-bound birds "coot-cicles." Bald eagles love them.

Adults are white-tailed, white-headed, yellow-billed, so that's easy. The four years between hatching and adulthood might be called the Long Blotch: juveniles are a scruffy mix of white and brown, and can be hard to tell from other big raptors. Compared to golden eagles, bald eagles always look shorter-tailed and bigger-headed. Juveniles also have white patches at the bases of their wings; golden eagles of all ages have dark armpits. Golden eagles are birds of high mountains and open deserts, while California's bald eagles mostly like reservoirs, big lakes, and the rivers and cliffs of the immediate coast—they breed on the Channel Islands, for example.

Bald eagles eat fish, ducks, carrion, and, in one famous clip circulating online, baby ospreys. Nests sit in the tops of tall snags and can be six, seven, even nine feet across. The female lays two (occasionally three) eggs. Chicks have voracious appetites—whoever coined the expression *You eat like a bird* hadn't studied an adolescent eagle. Nest cams remain popular and probably combine voyeurism with a genuine affection for nature. Expanding on that idea, maybe someday micro drones will follow the fledged eagle day and night, creating a sort of *Truman Show* of nonstop bird action. Until then, watch for them over deep reservoirs and along wild rivers, a symbol of freedom, majesty, and any other abstraction you want to stick onto them.

Northern Harrier   *Circus hudsonius*

🔭 marshes and open fields, including in the desert

Hovering and quartering, harriers work the marshland back and forth just above stalling speed, using their owl-like face discs and supersharp hearing to track down mice, voles, shrews, and birds. As hawks go, this one is easier than most. Long wings held in a shallow V, a long, ruddering tail, and a bold white rump patch all combine to confirm identification, no matter whether it's a female or young bird (which are brown) or the less commonly seen adult male (pale gray).

Harriers use all the hunting strategies in the book. When a rustle in the grass creates a point of interest, they can pull up short and hover like a kestrel, then drop and pounce with the fierce concentration of a leopard. Males are smaller than females, but since you usually see harriers as solo units, direct comparison is not very easy. What is true is that the male has black wing tips and a very pale underside, so combined with the gray body, it is one of our handsomest hawks.

Movements and ranges are complex. Found from Alaska to the Panama Canal, harriers fill in the entire North American map for at least one part of the year or another. (They are also widespread in Europe.) An open-country bird, harriers in California can be spotted coursing low over fresh and saltwater marshes, rice paddies, fallow fields, pastures, and meadows. They breed in the larger, more northerly wetlands in the state but also all the way down to Camp Pendleton in San Diego and Piute Ponds in the desert behind L.A.

This used to be called the marsh hawk, a fine and still-used name that is utterly appropriate. (Some changes in life are not for the better.) Attentive readers may have noticed the genus, *Circus*. Alas, no guy-wired big top, no acrobats in sequined tights, because it's just an adaption of the Greek word for hawk, *kirkos*.

Surely the planet will mend behind us as water heals
*   behind the canoe.*
—Connie Wanek

Cooper's Hawk *Accipiter cooperii*

👀 forests, woodlands, parks, cities

This is a midsized forest hawk that eats birds and small mammals, and it loves cities more than Woody Allen does. If we get past the folderol that claims Los Angeles is a concrete wasteland or that in Oakland there is no "there" there, the truth is that most California towns and cities are well-watered and well-forested. Trees line our streets, fill our parks, shade our backyards. Maybe we should have xeriscaped long ago, but cultural tastes didn't run that way historically, and now from San Diego to Bolinas, Bishop to Bakersfield, trees (both exotic and native) fill our skylines. In those trees are robins and mourning doves, sparrows and starlings, and streaking through the canopy and shooting across backyards are the bird hunters: Cooper's hawks, sharp-shinned hawks, and merlins.

Merlins are small, dark falcons that take sparrows and sandpipers. Cooper's and sharp-shinned hawks are both accipiters, a category of agile woodland raptor whose body plan includes broad, powerful wings and a rudder tail that lets them zag and zig after their justifiably panicked prey. Cooper's is the larger of the two, and it has made the transition to city life very successfully. They nest in downtown Berkeley, and I have seen one bullet through a parking lot in the middle of Hollywood, snatch a house sparrow, and disappear before you could say, "Who was that masked man?" You can see them in Death Valley (Furnace Creek Visitor Center), in the pines of Yosemite, or in your backyard…especially if you have a bird feeder swarming with goldfinches, sparrows, house finches, and juncos.

The old folk name was chicken hawk, with the invisible tag line *To be shot on sight*. We're more tolerant now (and marginally less ignorant), so nobody shotguns raptors. They do become ill from rat poison (as do bobcats, coyotes, and other "up the food chain" predators), and they can fly into windows, but it has become a very common urban bird. It was named early in the nineteenth century. William Cooper helped found the American Museum of Natural History in New York; the hawk was named for him by Charles Lucien Bonaparte, an associate of Audubon and Napoleon's nephew.

Juveniles (near left and below) are streakier and do not have the dark caps of adults (far left).

Red-shouldered Hawk   *Buteo lineatus*

👀 woodlands, forest edges, suburbia

If half of the bird list is well-named, the other half seems so misnamed that descriptions look as if they were created by a random word generator. Yes, while the red-shouldered hawk does have chestnut-red shoulders, the rest of the bird is that color too, not to mention overlays of stripes on the tail and black-and-white checkers dotted across the body. One ornithologist jokingly suggests naming it the zebra hawk, but an even better name would have been the crescent-winged hawk, due to the translucent crescent moons visible in flight.

The red-shouldered hawk is a compact predator, dense as a clenched fist. Short-winged and powerful, they can work inside the forest canopy, taking small mammals like rats, shrews, and squirrels, most midsized birds and sparrows, and whatever lizards, snakes, newts, and large insects wander into the range of their laser gaze. A bit to ornithology's surprise, it has successfully made the transition from the original habitat (cottonwood gallery forests) to modern life. From the Presidio to Point Reyes, from Camp Pendleton to Pomona, look for it now in backyards, along stream edges, on freeway margins, perched on power lines, and nesting on college campuses. It has crossed the Sierra and now occurs in Susanville, Reno, and the Owens Valley, while in the Bay Area, numbers rise each year, with vocal pairs often nesting in eucalyptus trees.

There is some variation in color patterns nationwide, with California birds being the reddest and most boldly patterned. In flight, the base of the primaries (the part of the wing about a third of the way in from the tip) shows a white crescent on each side, while a perched bird is a blend of stripes and checks on a reddish body. Loud and proud, for a hawk they can be quite noisy, nesting as early as December and calling *ki-eeeer ki-eeeer* over and over. Elsewhere in the US they can be migratory, but in California, once a pair claims a territory, they tend to stay put. As the bumper stickers claim: *Just another day in paradise.*

How we spend our days is, of course, how we spend our lives.—Annie Dillard

Red-tailed Hawk *Buteo jamaicensis*

👀 open country, mountains, everywhere else

Point to any distant, wheeling raptor and you can tell friends with confidence, "Oh look, there goes another red-tailed hawk." Law of averages, you'll be right. This one is our default hawk, seen on every UC campus and up and down the entire length of I-5 and in all nine of California's national parks, and most everywhere in between.

Imagine standing on the roof of your house or apartment and being able to read the date of a penny dropped on the sidewalk. Hawk sight is backed by speed and talons, and they eat more kinds of food than Anthony Bourdain. The list includes cats and dogs, rats and squirrels, voles and mice, snakes and lizards, grasshoppers and turtles, grackles and pheasants, crawdads and catfish. Habitat choices are equally broad: red-tails can be seen kiting in a stiff breeze over Catalina Island, perched on a light pole by a freeway, chasing jackrabbits in the high desert, skylining a ridgetop in the mountains, or circling with vultures, eagles, and condors over a dead whale at Big Sur.

The "tail" part of the name is accurate, but only most of the time. The diagnostic cinnamon color is easiest to pick out from above, as the hawk makes a banking turn, and is hardest to see when backlit from below. The chest often has a row of up-and-down hash marks, scribbled and variable, though in fact the whole package is variable, from all-black versions to the palest, whitest ones. Seen from below, the leading edge of the wing has a dark band from the neck to the halfway mark, and usually the wing ends in outstretched fingers (the primaries).

We see so many liveries in part because we see so many red-tailed hawks period; in terms of straight numbers, this is the commonest, most abundant hawk in the American West.

The hawk's cry is as sharp as its beak.
—Edward Abbey

An adult (above) gathers nesting material. A young bird (right) does not yet show full color in its tail.

Golden Eagle *Aquila chrysaetos*

 open country, especially deserts and mountains

Deserts and mountains provide the backdrop for seeing golden eagles, but its huge wings seem to fill the whole sky, no matter how wide or how blue. Roman, German, and French armies have all marched under imperial eagle banners; Genghis Khan flew golden eagles as falconry birds. They can take down a sandhill crane or catch a coyote, fox, or even a wolf, and so in the Sierra and the California deserts, golden eagles count as the king of kings on the food pyramid.

We have two strands of eagle populations in California; the year-round ones live and breed here, moving down from the Sierra high country when snow makes game harder to find. Winter sees the rest arrive in a migration wave of golden eagles coming from the Great Basin and Alaska. When DDT caused the Channel Islands to lose their native bald eagles, golden eagles flew over to take up residency. That in turn almost drove the endemic island foxes to extinction. Since then the golden eagles have been relocated to the mainland; fish-eating bald eagles have been reintroduced; and the foxes scamper with joy.

These birds are titled "golden" not for "worth their weight in" but from a drape of yellowy tan running crown to neck. (In California, even the birds want to be blonds.) The only thing bigger and more voracious than an eagle is a wind turbine. In the past, Altamont Pass was a giant sausage grinder when it came to raptors, its turbines killing fifty to one hundred eagles a year. Changing the height, placement, design, and seasons of use for the turbines can help a lot; new, more efficient designs are now being phased in.

Sad but true: green energy is rarely completely green, and the cleanest energy of all is just to turn off your iPhone and go for a walk.

I know he'd be a poor man if he never saw an eagle fly.
—John Denver

Even a young eagle (left) is huge and powerful.

Barn Owl *Tyto alba*

 marshes, fields, deserts, woodlands, suburbia (sometimes)

Nature designs special features for a reason, and the barn owl's round, smooshed-in face is no exception. The entire face is one giant reflecting dish, while asymmetrical ears help give its hearing perfect triangulation. It can hear—and catch—a mouse in total darkness. Once it zeroes in on a target, supersoft flight feathers allow it to glide in for the kill as quietly as a snowflake settling on a tray of cotton balls.

The barn owl's range includes North and South America, as well as much of the Old World. Since they like open ground, airports are good hunting zones: one arrived in New Zealand by getting caught up in the landing gear of a 747 as it took off in Australia. Barn owls do nest in barns and steeples and other human buildings, but also in palm trees, on cliff edges, in holes in the sheer sides of riverbanks, and just inside cave entrances. One folk belief says that if you hear an owl calling, somebody will die soon. Another says you can cancel that by taking off your right shoe and turning it upside down. (For how long? Sources don't say.) All owls have amazing night vision—much better than ours—yet can see fine in daytime too. Alas, an oncoming truck's high beams may disorient them, and one sad reality is it's very easy to find roadkilled barn owls along the margins of busy highways.

Females are tawnier than males, but at night both look very pale; typically you expect them on rural roads around old meadows and homesteads. Besides being ghostly white in headlights, barn owls add to the haunted-house effect because they don't go *hoo, hoo* but instead just moan and hiss. Their usual song sounds like somebody slowly opening a creaky door, or maybe it's more like a hoarse kitten complaining about being made to endure a long, cold bath. However you transcribe it, it's not a pretty sound. Generally, though, this

is a silent hunter, seen lifting off a fence post when you're driving late at night in the countryside.

> To make an owl
> is to forget yourself,
> the coins in your pockets,
> failed love,
> the fame you'll never have.
> —Tom Crawford

Great Horned Owl *Bubo virginianus*

👀 forests, deserts, marshes, city parks

Widespread in urban and natural habitats, this finely striped, cat-eared night bird is the easiest of our fourteen owls to see. You might hear one in a park, or see it fly across the marsh at dusk, or come across one at midday in an abandoned barn, and each time it's like meeting an old friend (even if you've never seen one before). *Whoo-hooting* full voice in the cold, still dusk of February, great horned owls nest early in the spring and want the world to know that their territory is *theirs*.

Paired owls share in defending territories, though the nest is rebuilt fresh each year and in the nonbreeding season they may go their own ways, roosting and hunting separately. Is that the secret to a happy marriage? Separate bedrooms and long vacations away from the kids? Great horned owls eat prey as small as crickets and shrews (things that barely weigh more than a few raisins), but they usually try for midsized rations: rabbits, squirrels, cats, skunks, and even herons and ducks.

Looking for pellets—their coughed up hairballs of fur and bone—may help you find an owl, since pellets accumulate under roost trees (see page 79). Dissecting a pellet lets us discover what a hawk or owl has been eating. In California, that's a lot, since our owls come in all sizes and live in all different habitats. Some owls eat moths; others, like the burrowing owl and short-eared owl, hunt from (and rest on) the ground; the elf owl along the Colorado River nests in saguaro cactus. If you have access to Doctor Who's TARDIS, ask him to take you back to the winter of 1896, when Northern California was filled with (direct quote) "flocks" of snowy owls. We've had over fifty snowy owl records since then, yet another thing to hope to come across on a fine winter morning.

Write it on your heart that every day is the best day in the year.
—Ralph Waldo Emerson

Burrowing Owl *Athene cunicularia*

👓 deserts and fields; most common at the Salton Sea

Within earshot of planes landing at LAX, the Ballona Wetlands are home to a strange and wonderful owl. It has bright yellow eyes and a sandy brown vest crosshatched with chestnut-red squiggles. This is the petite but feisty burrowing owl, and it lives on the ground in small family groups. It comes out not just at night but also during the day, standing on top of squirrel mounds and peering around like a wide-awake toddler.

Its grandstand need not be huge. Small elevations suit them, and you may well glimpse a burrowing owl perched on top of a bush surveying its small kingdom. (If you go to the savannahs of Brazil, they'll be on top of termite mounds.) Like other owls, they can swivel their heads in a surprising range, so the body can stay still while the head revolves around like a doll in a horror film. The name is slightly misleading: it is less of a *burrowing* owl and more of a *borrowing* owl, since it often inhabits tunnels pre-dug by ground squirrels or badgers or rabbits.

These owls eat lizards, snakes, frogs, mice, gophers, grasshoppers, beetles, and baby birds, and were initially common up and down the state. Compact but efficient hunters, they have selected a good target prey size, and in the past their ground-based lifestyle was a clever choice. After all, you might run out of trees, but there's always open ground. Now you will need to go to the Salton Sea to see oodles, with just remnant last-stands elsewhere, such as east of King City or the ones at Ballona. Life is hard for all of us, birds included, and these days burrowing owls can get sick from rat poison, can have their burrows raided by snakes, can be hassled by stray dogs, or can just wake up one morning to hear bulldozers and see a sign: *Future Home of Walmart.*

Those that remain help remind us not to be too complacent. Yes, we "know" owls always live in trees and hunt at night—except when they live by the beach and hunt during the day. As the poet Walt Whitman says, "Do I contradict myself? Very well then I contradict myself."

Owl Pellets

Love the animals, love the plants, love everything.
—*Fyodor Dostoyevsky*

Owls can't digest bones and fur, so they cough up leftovers in a gray oval called a pellet. (Eagles and hawks spit these up too.) Look for pellets under roost trees, such as tall, dense pines in a city park. If you find pellets, you can break them open in order to find out what the owl has been eating. (They are not stinky or poo-like, though be sure to wash up afterward.)

Tiny mouse jaws with tiny mouse teeth are oh-so-cute, while shiny pieces of pale green shell reveal that the owl has been snacking on scorpions. Tibia and ribs are easy to name; other fragments provide a harder *CSI* puzzle. Depending how much rain has fallen, many weeks' worth of pellets can accumulate inside barns, along cliff berms, and under roost trees, so if you find a pile of owl pellets on the ground, look up to see if the owner is home. He or she might be sleeping directly above your head.

Before and after shots of a great horned owl pellet show the mouse bones hidden within.

Food in, pellets out: a young (and rain-drenched) red-tailed hawk listens for voles.

Usually nocturnal, great horned owls also hunt in daylight when feeding their young.

Belted Kingfisher *Megaceryle alcyon*

🔭 rivers, lakes, ponds, bays

A rattled call, a bolt of slate from above, a piercing dive into calm water, and—off it goes!—the kingfisher has taken another fish and shot off to a nearby snag to flip it around and swallow it headfirst. If "piscivore" means fish-eater, what would be the word for "attractively colored, big-headed, long-billed, mohawk-crested fish-eater"? Both males and females are belted, in that they have a slate band across the top of the chest, but in a reversal of gender displays, only females sport a second chestnut band across the all-white tummy. Burrow nesters, kingfishers need a sheer earth bank to dig into, such as an embankment cut by a river, or the sides of a gravel quarry. Territories may be linear: up and down the stream but not much past it. Though they do eat lizards and even fruit, they want to control prime fishing spots. "Locals only," as the surfers say, and for kingfishers, local means mister and missus, nobody else.

It almost looks like a large, demented blue jay, but jays never dive for fish, and no tern would be blue and crested. Terns overlap with kingfishers in bays and harbors (less so, rivers and inland lakes), but once you see a kingfisher, you won't have any doubt about what it is. Some do stay to breed, but most of our population comes in winter (July to April), and they are more common north to south yet even present in eastern California deserts—especially if there's a nearby backyard fishpond.

The kingfisher was once a minor goddess and the daughter of the wind god Aeolus, who, for seven days out of the year, calmed the winds so that his daughter might lay her eggs in peace. Thank this bird for our Indian summers—those wind-free, halcyon days—even in downtown San Francisco.

Kingfishers can be seen at the Sepulveda Basin Wildlife Reserve, adjacent to some of the busiest freeways in the United States.

Acorn Woodpecker *Melanerpes formicivorus*

👓 oak woodlands, city parks

Meet the foothills' clown-faced oak specialist. Loud, communal, strikingly colored, and loyal to tribal clans—such attributes either describe the acorn woodpecker or else trekkers leaving Burning Man. An acorn woodpecker's *whacka-whacka-whacka* call can be heard throughout the day, and allegedly inspired the laugh of the cartoon Woody Woodpecker.

Most woodpeckers are black and white; acorn woodpeckers are too, but with this species the red head and pale eyes add to the bold effect. White patches on the wings flash bright in shade or sun, and the roller coaster flight—flap and glide, flap and glide—is both distinctive and easy to notice. Although not

> *The creation of a thousand forests is in one acorn.*
> *—Ralph Waldo Emerson*

attracted to people, they don't avoid us either. They are active all day long, patrolling territories centered on granaries. Granaries are trees, telephone poles, or even the sides of barns—any substrate into which acorn-sized holes can be chiseled by the woodpeckers' sharp beaks. Family groups share these central repositories, gathering acorns during the fall and hammering them into place for retrieval later. A single granary tree may hold 10,000 acorns (or at least have 10,000 acorn-sized holes). Find the acorns and you'll find the birds, which can be high, low, or in between: they forage on the ground, perch midway up the tree, or scan for insects from the very crown of the tree, almost always yakking back and forth raucously.

Oak trees supply their main food. Yosemite Valley is a good place to watch for your first ones, but they are found in many places. If you want to combine birding with outdoor sports, the world's oldest disc golf course is near Pasadena at Hahamongna Watershed Park; the oaks there almost always have acorn woodpeckers (and other foothill birds besides).

Northern Flicker *Colaptes auratus*

....

👀 woodlands, city parks, sometimes lawns and golf courses

Big and brown and spotted, this woodpecker nests in trees but forages on the ground, and is the least fussy of any North American woodpecker. Golf courses and cemeteries and parks; oak trees and pine forests: it's all the same this bird. Its flight is a swoopy, roller-coastered flap and glide, showing off red underwings, and its loud *kyeer* call can carry across even a large park. A black cravat separates plain head from spotted chest; seen closely, males have a smear of red across each cheek, like a kid caught eating a jam tart.

Trees are used to drum signal calls, while derelict flicker nest holes are perfect for kestrels and small owls. To increase the racket, some flickers (apparently unconcerned about headaches later) drum not on trees but metal objects.

Of 132 recorded folk names for the flicker, how about the harrywicket? That sounds rustic yet cultivated, like something from a lawn bowling tournament. Some books (and birders) still call ours the red-shafted flicker, since there's a yellow-winged one in the eastern U.S.A. that once was listed as a separate species. The shafts of the western flicker's feathers are indeed a translucent orangey red, and tail and wing feathers have red vanes. They were used by Native Americans in dance regalia, body ornaments, and basketry. Capture choices varied; some tribes ate flickers, getting dinner and headband in one trip to the woods, while others caught flickers in traps, culled a few select feathers, and released the birds afterward. It's an easy feather to notice and identify, and since flickers are common and since all birds molt, you can find stray feathers just while hiking, or, as I did once, in front of a mansion in Pasadena.

Do not fear literary critics; they are just woodpeckers. The more diseased the tree, the happier they are.
—Mark Yakich

American Kestrel *Falco sparverius*

👀 open country, fields, urban edges

A kestrel is a peregrine falcon for your vest pocket, and each nation-state deserves to have one. Few other creatures are as inspiring or as dapper in all sexes and plumages and yet as willing to make a living out of freeway berms and abandoned farmland.

An older name for the kestrel is a sparrow hawk, and they do take sparrows, along with lizards, mice, small snakes, and even bats. As with most other raptors, female kestrels are larger than males, which some theorists think protects nestlings (ain't nothin' gonna mess with mama), or else maybe helps the pair partition resources: in lean times, at least one of the parent birds is bound to be suited for catching whatever's surplus. Or it could be that the female needs to accumulate more energy before laying eggs, like a car topping off the gas tank before crossing the desert. Or maybe, because they are smaller and hence more nimble, males are ever-so-slightly better providers when mom's stuck on nest duty. Or maybe none of these guesses is the right one, and it will be up to the next generation of grad students to find newer, better answers.

Display flights are suitably dramatic. When claiming breeding territory, male kestrels climb high into the air, call from the top of the arc, and dive, then rise up to do it again, each time crying out *kleee kleee*. Great drama inspires great art: Jesuit poet Gerard Manley Hopkins wrote an exuberant, intoxicating poem about kestrels called "The Windhover." (The fewer footnotes you read for that text, the more sense it will make.)

In poetry and in life, kestrels are so buoyant they seem to run on a mixture of jet fuel and champagne. Whether hovering over a vole run or beating across a meadow to chase down a sparrow, the kestrel reminds us that we don't need big country and sheer cliffs to make a living. Sometimes just an old tree, a stretch of dried grass, and half a dozen grasshoppers will do.

If I had to choose, I would rather have birds than airplanes.—Charles Lindbergh

A female (above) is larger than a male, with a chestnut back; males show more blue-gray.

Peregrine Falcon *Falco peregrinus*

🔭 mountain cliffs, estuaries, rocky coastline

Screamingly fast, the peregrine is the Top Gun of the avian world. One of the folk names, duck hawk, is about a thousand times too slow—yes, they'll take ducks, but with 240-mile-per-hour dives, peregrines can chase down anything in the sky, even white-throated swifts. Eggshell thinning linked to DDT poisoning once nearly made them extinct, but changes in pesticide laws and an active program of captive breeding and releasing the fledged young birds (often in the middle of pigeon-filled cities) helped bring them back from the edge of oblivion. Even now, some ego-deficit yahoo is screaming his Bugatti Veyron up Highway 1—and looking down, bemused, a peregrine falcon is thinking, "What a poseur. That isn't fast; *this* is fast," as it takes off on another hunting foray.

The clearest way into the Universe is through a forest wilderness.
—John Muir

They eat everything from sparrows to egrets. A dive is called a "stoop"; the peregrine smashes into the prey with clenched fists, and as the now-dead duck or pigeon tumbles earthward, the peregrine flies underneath, flips around, grabs it, and flies off to pluck and eat.

Falcons don't look like hawks. Perched, the peregrine has a blue hood; in flight, narrow wings and a fast, rowing beat create a very different profile. To see your first peregrine, look at the smokestacks of Monterey Bay Aquarium as your whale-watching boat comes back into port—that's a traditional perch—or else go to the Palo Alto wetlands at dawn. Be ready, and at the exact moment every killdeer, duck, godwit, whimbrel, and savannah sparrow bolts for cover, look up to glimpse a peregrine shooting through the marsh like a dark blue meteor. Morro Rock usually has a pair of peregrines (and sometimes two pairs).

With skyscraper ledges being just as good as cliffs, they nest in downtown L.A. and San Jose, and they can once again be seen statewide, from the North American Wall on El Capitan to the Coronado Bay Bridge in San Diego. Falconers love this species (and generally only use captive-bred birds); tame or wild, near or far, any peregrine on the wing is worth waiting for.

Each year, peregrines nest on Morro Rock near San Luis Obispo.

Red-crowned Parrot *Amazona viridigenalis*

👀 tropical trees in Southern California

The *Amazona* group includes a constellation of stunners—red-crowned, lilac-crowned, blue-fronted, white-fronted, yellow-headed, red-lored (the lores are the area of a bird's face between eye and beak). All are native to the American tropics, and all occur in Southern California as free-flying, wild birds. These are not the same as the parrots of Telegraph Hill; those are red-masked parakeets, also known as cherry-headed conures. Some of those are in L.A. too, as well as San Diego.

There may be as many red-crowned parrots in L.A. and Orange Counties as are left in their home range in Mexico. (They also live in San Diego and Florida.) Like many other parrots they are cavity nesters, and when feeding in a tree they can be quiet and blend in fully. See them flying in pairs or small, screechy flocks; the red-crowned parrot is a chunky, short-tailed parrot, with a yellow tail, red cap, and blue-and-red wing panels. We've made our yards and cities so lushly subtropical it's no wonder they thrive here—they can nest, feed, and hide from predators, sometimes in the exact same species of trees as they would have encountered in their home rain forests. As Axl Rose sings, "Welcome to the jungle."

Why parrots, why here? California was part of a large, now-condemned pet trade, so that as late as the 1960s one could walk into a store and buy a baby monkey or a wild-caught parrot. We no longer allow that, but enough parrots were in circulation that escapees became established as free-flying birds, now numbering in the thousands. Evening roosts are raucous and can be found in several South Pasadena and San Gabriel Valley neighborhoods. People who complain about the noise (and droppings) should just be glad that New Zealand's crow-sized kea parrot was never released here. It has a bill like an oversized can opener and likes to investigate cars by peeling away the rubber around windows or cutting through soft-tops of convertibles. They also fly off with things—including (at least once) a man's passport.

In comparison, California's parrots just want to eat all the blossoms on your tree and will gladly ignore your identity papers.

To see parrots, first listen: they'll announce themselves if they're around.

Yellow-chevroned Parakeet *Brotogeris chiriri*

🔭 tropical trees in Southern California

One way to think about California is as a rugged, wild, Guinness World Records gallery of native diversity—home of the giant sequoia, by volume the largest living thing on the planet; and also of some of the oldest trees, bristlecone pines; and the biggest animals, blue and fin and humpback whales. But seen another way, California is now also a landscape of altered, blended, and reinvented ecology, with many dozens of newcomers permanently resident and thriving here, from the wild turkey to the wild pig to rainbow trout to most people themselves. And not just cockroaches and starlings are non-native: Peruvian pepper trees now grow wild, as do eucalyptus trees and Mexican fan palms and the ailanthus, or tree of heaven. Even most of our honeybees and ants came here from elsewhere.

Screeching overhead, yellow-chevroned parakeets embody this principle completely. According to the clichés, Los Angeles should not be home to much of anything other than maybe some dazed TV has-beens with Sunday-morning hangovers, or their entrepreneurial counterparts, the hawkers at off-ramps selling maps to the homes of stars. Yet the list of Southern California trees includes the silk floss, a type of ceiba tree related to the sacred origin tree of the Ancient Maya and to the kapok tree, whose cotton-fiber seedpods helped fill Allied life jackets in World War II. Yellow-chevroned parakeets love silk floss trees but also can be seen in palm trees and eucalyptus trees, or any of a thousand other tropical species. Listen for these birds when bringing out-of-town guests to Getty Villa or the Huntington's botanical gardens, or see them shooting by like air-show jets when you're biking along the L.A. River.

To learn more about this bird or its closely related look-alike, the white-winged parakeet, or any other of a dozen local psittacine marvels, there's a very good website run by the California Parrot Project. Parakeet populations are still expanding (or, for some species, contracting); if you want to help out, America needs more parrot watchers.

A parakeet investigates the pod on a silk floss tree (far left). One owner's loss is a new flock's beginning (left).

Rose-ringed Parakeet   *Psittacula krameri*

👀 city parks (mostly in Bakersfield)

Four cities: London, Amsterdam, Brussels, and Bakersfield. Of these, Bakersfield has more of something than any of the others, and it's not just oil derricks or Buck Owens tribute bands. All four have introduced populations of the rose-ringed parakeet, but the flocks in Bakersfield are now at 3,000 and rising. In the US, other, smaller colonies can be found in Florida, Texas, and Los Angeles, but Bakersfield remains the top rose-ringed parakeet site in California and in the nation. Does the chamber of commerce know? Maybe it could become the official city mascot.

This is a long-tailed, bright green parrot from India (or at least it was from India originally). Only the males have a black-and-pink ring around the neck, but both males and females are large, visible, gorgeous animals. In Bakersfield they come home at night to communal roosts (try Hart Park) and disperse during the day to feed. Strong flyers, they can travel far to feed in a variety of trees, eating fruit, seeds, nuts, berries, and flower buds. Beaks are red, sharp, and dexterous: don't let one bite you or you risk losing a finger.

How did they get out of their cages in the first place? In 1977 hurricane-force winds ripped the roof off an aviary in Bakersfield. The happy inmates took two deep breaths and promptly skedaddled. Later, those founder parakeets located each other and had babies, plus every year a few more pets got loose, and soon a handful of parakeets became a full tree's worth, outward and onward, until we now have thousands of free-roaming parakeets. In ecological terms, the population has become "naturalized." How natural or unnatural it is may be a matter of debate, but so far they are doing okay. Their motto seems to be *Bakersfield today, Visalia tomorrow, and the rest of the world the day after that.*

Black Phoebe   *Sayornis nigricans*

👀 city parks, backyards, streams near woodlands

Such an easy bird to like, this tuxedo-sporting flycatcher. It has no middle-of-the-night alarm calls, so it's not a mockingbird. It doesn't swarm over crops, so it's not a starling. It's not hiding in the deepest part of the bush, so it's not a thrasher. Instead, it's in your backyard, over the lawns of your nearest college, by a marshy pond, or in a well-watered city park, always waiting patiently and then zipping up from a bench or low branch to catch a day-flying moth, smack it once or twice on a rock, and gobble it down. Its name rhymes with "freebie."

Male and female, old and young, patterns stay the same: black head, black body, black tail, black beak, black eyes, and an all-white belly. It has good posture: alert as a cocked gun. Like other flycatchers, it makes short flights across the yard to catch (or miss) a passing insect. It usually comes back to land on a new perch twenty or fifty feet away, or sometimes just goes back to where it started. The tail wags up and down like somebody using a hand pump to fill a bucket. Why does the tail do that? Theories include maintaining balance, warming up for hunting, claiming territory, breaking up a static profile to create a confusing shape, or (and this could be the right one) it signals to predators that the phoebe is attentive and ready. When phoebes hear or see a predator like a Cooper's hawk, the tail really gets going. That in turn advertises the phoebe's ability to dart zippity zip out of the way, telling the hawk it's not worth it—the phoebe will always get away, like Roadrunner outwitting Wile E. Coyote.

It's mostly found in California, Arizona, and New Mexico, though black phoebes also live in Mexico and in a narrow ribbon down through the Andes.

A black phoebe has a dragonfly (right) but seems unsure what to do next.

Say's Phoebe *Sayornis saya*

Like kingbirds and black phoebes and vermilion flycatchers, the Say's phoebe is a sit-and-scan predator, darting out to snatch a passing moth or grasshopper. (It also takes insects from the ground.) And like the black phoebe, it will come into parks and backyards, but unlike that one, the Say's phoebe prefers deserts and sagebrush empires, avoiding rivers and soggy lawns and closed-in woodlands.

Grayish brown, darker above than below, it shows a wash of tan from between the legs to undertail. Since it's smaller than a kingbird but larger, more out-in-the-open-ish than the all-drab empids and peewees, it helps you learn other flycatchers. It's another tail pumper, and like the black phoebe it has a thin, insect-catching (not conical and seed-crunching) bill. The color pattern looks a bit like a California towhee's but the towhee's posture is more horizontal (versus a flycatcher's up-and-down, ready-for-battle pose), and the towhee is a ground feeder that hops forward and back, scratching seeds into view. Say's phoebes might hunt from the ground (though more typically it's from a fence post or branch), but if so, they always sally up to find an insect, and have only minimal interest in the salad bar.

Thomas Say was a mid-nineteenth-century naturalist who named over a thousand species of beetles; it seems a little ironic that a beetle-eating bug-snatcher memorializes him.

Vermilion Flycatcher   *Pyrocephalus rubinus*

👀 desert oases (in winter, rare in parks)

It will be said only once in this book, but it really is true: pictures can't do justice to the amazing cha-cha-cha redness of a male vermilion flycatcher. It is mostly a summer visitor (though a few linger into winter), and when you find one, you will see how it lights up the air like a very small, very intense red sun.

In body plan it's the same as other small flycatchers, including the Say's and black phoebes. Like those two, it perches upright on the tips of branches, on fence posts and snags, or even on playground equipment, flying a quick sortie to nab a moth or grasshopper, then coming back to a new perch nearby. Also like them, it flicks its tail in an absent-minded sort of pumping or dipping. However, in the vermilion flycatcher the sexes differ very strongly: males are red and black but females and juveniles are dull gray with a pink wash.

In California the usual place to spot them is Big Morongo Canyon near Palm Springs, though it breeds sometimes in the Kern County deserts, and very rarely even in L.A. Displaying males puff themselves up and flutter like drunken butterflies. In winter both adults and juveniles spread themselves across the Southern California map, with a dozen or so sightings split between cemeteries and urban parks and the Colorado River and Salton Sea. If one is around, it will be reported on the rare bird alerts.

In Spanish the name is *mosquero cardenal,* "cardinal flycatcher"—though this guy is even brighter red than a cardinal (the eastern bird or the kind in the Vatican), and the black eye line makes the scarlet crown even more vivid. We know better than to wish for a change in the ecological balance, but even so, if this species were to become just a *teensy* bit more widespread, not many people would complain.

When I haven't any blue I use red.—Pablo Picasso

Females and juveniles mix pink and gray; males (above) glow bright red.

Western Kingbird   *Tyrannus verticalis*

👀 ranches, open country, city parks

If we were to appoint an honorary mayor of abandoned ranches and rest stops, it would be the western kingbird.

Western kingbirds are easiest seen (and heard, *bik, bik, bik, bik*) near open areas like fields, prairies, parks, and picnic ramadas, particularly in the drier parts of the state. No matter how hot the day or how bleak the asphalt, these lemon-bellied bug-zappers sally forth from posts or branches to snatch grasshoppers, wasps, bees, and beetles out of the air or off the ground. Once they grab a prey item, they loop back to their perch, whacking the bug until it's subdued. How many until it feels full? In 1869 a kingbird named Chippy ate 120 grasshoppers in one day, having been fed them, one by one, by bored soldiers on an expedition in Utah.

Western kingbirds are a bit smaller than a robin. Both males and females share the yellow-tummy, gray-backed pattern. Seen closely, the tip of the bill has a small hook, not hooked enough to open an old-fashioned can of beer, but just enough to remind us that this guy takes on hornets for a living. When it comes to their bird neighbors, kingbirds reveal an odd mixture of tolerance and NIMBYism. They are content to share nest trees with doves or sparrows, but if a crow or hawk strays into their no-fly zone it will be escorted off the premises tout de suite.

A summer visitor to California, this species is on duty April through September, when it takes off for the tropics. It is replaced in winter (especially along the coast) by the slightly stockier Cassin's kingbird, which has a whiter throat and darker outer tail feathers. That one is named for John Cassin, a nineteenth-century Quaker businessman and naturalist who sailed with Commodore Perry and died from arsenic poisoning, a by-product of a lifetime of preparing bird specimens. Unlike their summer cousins, Cassin's kingbirds sometimes form small flocks, and besides insects they will also eat berries and wild grapes, all of which we hope are organic and arsenic-free.

A ranch yard with cottonwoods is perfect kingbird territory.

Loggerhead Shrike *Lanius ludovicianus*

👀 open country, fields, desert

Think of a shrike as a mockingbird that plans to be a hawk when it grows up. For a songbird (its technical classification) it is a surprisingly fierce hunter. Mice, sparrows, snakes, grasshoppers—the hooked bill and

How brightly you whistle, pushing the long soft feathers on your rump down across the branch, like the apron of a butcher, as you impale a cricket on a meat hook deep inside my rhododendron.
—Henri Cole

harpoon-quick flight help it take things nearly as big as the shrike itself. Any spare food is kabobbed onto a barbed wire fence or long thorn or sharp branch, to be eaten later. This gap between catching and eating toxic prey, like a monarch butterfly, allows poisons to break down; a well-stocked cache also may advertise to ladies what a handy breadwinner the male can be. Who needs a Ferrari when you've got a plump day-old mouse?

This is a clean, sleek bird, and if it poses just right the black face mask lines up with the black beak and black wings, creating a crisp divide between the pale gray back and white underside. To hunt, it waits on a perch with a good view—maybe a fence post or a Joshua tree or an isolated bush. When it's time to strike, it jets off, and if it's successful, it brings the trophy home, carried in beak or claws depending how small or big it is.

Shrikes prefer open country—especially grasslands, pastures, and deserts—and even though the American West seems to be nothing but open country, they have been declining year by year. There seem to be multiple causes, including an increase in car traffic, houses replacing fields, and our massive reliance on pesticides, which decreases insect diversity. In the US, they do better in the west than the east, where they have become truly rare.

According to poet Robert Hass, the expression "to be at loggerheads" relates to sailors fighting with the brass balls used to soften a pail of tar. A secondary meaning has to do with being a blockhead, literally or figuratively. This swift hunter is no more bumble-witted than many other things in the world, nor does it have a particularly large head. As usual, the common name says more about us than it does about the creature.

Steller's Jay *Cyanocitta stelleri*

 forests (coastal or montane), piney yards

Scrub-jays (next entry) fill the lowlands, but this is California's *other* jay: still loud, still curious, but all-blue and with a peaked crest and a preference for pine and fir trees. You can hear this species coming from half a forest away as it yells out its screechy *sheek, sheeeek,* and if you're camping or having a lunch stop, their potato chip radar alerts them the minute you open the trunk.

The Steller's jay is a forest or heavy woodland bird throughout its range. In Central and Northern California, forest often comes right down to the sea, and so does the Steller's jay. In Southern California, most woodland is confined to higher elevations and shady canyons, limiting the Steller's jay to the high country. There are exceptions; Steller's jays overlap with scrub-jays along stream courses and in some of the denser oak forests, and in foothill cities like Pasadena that have a lot of pine trees.

Steller's jays eat acorns, bird eggs, trash, and anything that catches their eye. They do cache seeds for later, and they'll also raid any squirrel larders they discover. They come happily to backyard feeders, but there's some concern that if artificial food sources inflate populations, their appetite for eggs might impact the populations of smaller woodland species trying to nest nearby. As a footnote of avian trivia, none of the blue jays are blue. They *look* blue, but the actual feathers are brown: the blue is structural, caused by the way light enters (and is backscattered by) the cell structures of the feather barbs themselves.

The common and Latin names commemorate an early naturalist, Georg Steller. He was a German doctor who was shipwrecked with explorer Vitus Bering on the Siberian coast. Bering died and Steller lived, in part because Steller intuited that eating moss counteracted scurvy. Many animals and birds are named for him, including a now-extinct Alaskan manatee called the Steller's sea cow.

The world is blue at its edges and in its depths. This blue is the light that got lost.
—Rebecca Solnit

California Scrub-Jay *Aphelocoma californica*

👀 brush, woodlands, parks, yards

North America once had only one scrub jay, but then closer looks at their ecology and social structure helped change that, and now we have four species. All follow the same body plan: blue above, gray below, with a small gray shoulder cape and a blue chest band like a badge of office for a small European country. Fierce intelligence and bold curiosity mean they want to know *everything* about your campsite. What are you eating? What will you do with that trash? What happens if they tug on your wiper blades?

Oaks give this lanky, long-tailed bird the acorns it depends on, but the California scrub-jay explores a broad range of habitats, from grasslands to rest areas on 101

Our observations depend on our questions.—Ernst Gombrich

to Joshua tree woodlands to the golf courses at Pebble Beach. Most typically it is a mid-altitude species, found in chaparral and scrubby forest, and moving in loose, noisy flocks that announce themselves with a screechy *jree, jree* that is easy to learn (if hard to imitate and even harder to transcribe). Besides picnic scraps and acorns, this scrub-jay also eats bees, crickets, ticks, wild and domestic fruit, mice, lizards, and bird eggs.

Our blue jay is not the blue jay of eastern North America (which only occurs here as a rare stray), but even so, we've got plenty of jays to spare. An all-gray jay lives in north-western California (the gray jay or whiskyjack), a powder-blue jay *peents* through piñon forests (the pinyon jay), and for the piney woods kind, all-blue and preferring the forest canopy, see the previous entry, Steller's jay.

When bored with those choices, South Texas has both a brown jay and a bright green jay, and, closer to home, sometimes around San Diego one sees escaped pets, the magpie-jays.

Yellow-billed Magpie *Pica nuttalli*

👀 oak woodlands, grasslands, parks

Not the California quail, not the California condor, not the California scrub-jay, but this one—*this* species should be our state bird, since it's found nowhere else in the world. (An earlier name was "California magpie.")

High in a tall tree, the nest looks like a big tangled mass of mistletoe. Like jays and crows, magpies eat roadkill, insects, fruit, worms, eggs, and human trash. They can be seen in orchards and pastures as well as in their natural oak savannas. Conversion of old fields and oak scrub into row after row of wine grapes may be good for future sommeliers, but it ultimately leaves fewer places for magpies, shrews, honeybees, and titmice. Magpies adapt to marginal and suburban habitats to some degree (another trait they share with crows and jays), but were also badly hit in the aughts by West Nile virus. It's tough to be a wild critter in the modern world.

Like other corvids, they're bright mimics, and from back when we kept wild animals as ranch pets, there's a story of a magpie that learned how to say all the words to stop and start a horse team. It would rile up the whole barnyard with its "whoas" and "gee haw now" commands, as the owner chased the stock back and forth, trying to hitch up the wagon.

Long tail, yellow bill, and white wing flashes make this snappy fellow a dead-easy bird to identify, and once you've dialed in your first one, you'll start to see them lots of places, such as flying across 101 north of Paso Robles or around campus at UC Davis. A second species, the black-billed magpie, is closely related and lives east of the Sierra in the Owens Valley and the far northeast corner of the state.

It's morning, and again I am
that lucky person who is in it.
—Mary Oliver

The black-billed magpie (below) is a sister species from the Owens Valley. It has a black, not yellow, bill.

American Crow *Corvus brachyrhynchos*

🔭 beaches, towns, fields, dumps, parks, orchards

Crows are smaller and "townier" than ravens, with square tails and a nasal *caw, caw*. Both species are all-black and brainiac smart. In crows, the bill is more like a pair of pliers than like a raven's broadax schnoz, and crows look tidy and sleek, never shaggy. Crows usually avoid harsh extremes: orchards and city parks, yes, but no summer deserts for them, thank you very much.

As do ravens and jays, crows eat bird eggs. This makes them the bad guys according to some, but from a biological perspective they are merely being true to their natural appetites. Everything interests them, from salamanders to grapes to garbage to the leftover corn once a field has been picked. Crows even like to explore tide pools. How do you eat a sea urchin? Fly high over the parking lot, drop it, watch it smash. You can also take mussels and arrange them in a line on the pavement so cars drive over them, doing the smashing for you.

Crows are talkative, social birds. In winter they roost in dense flocks—look for them at dusk along Highway 99, for example, coming from as far as fifty miles away to gather in roadside eucalyptus trees. It may seem ominous, but it isn't. The usual noun of assemblage for this species is a *murder* of crows, but poet Charles Goodrich suggests a new name, honoring what nature can teach us: a *scripture* of crows.

Why call it the "American" crow? The distinction matters. Europe has a carrion crow, India has a house crow, and in the US, three other crows look similar to this one. They include the fish crow, the northwestern crow, and the Tamaulipas crow, a Mexican species found only in Texas at the Brownsville dump. If you want to know where on the scale you fit between normal birdwatcher and hard-core birder, ask yourself what you would pay not to have to go there and look for it.

The best way to get on a crow's good side is through its stomach.—Jennifer Campbell-Smith

Common Raven *Corvus corax*

👀 mountains, deserts, dumps, rocky coastline

Ravens are clever, beefy, and built for action. Compared with crows, the raven is harsher-voiced, shaggier-coated, broader-winged, wider-ranging. Both species like dumps, but crows stick to towns and orchards while ravens take nature as it comes, from summer deserts to winters in the Sierra high country. Ravens circle on thermals with hawks (crows don't), and ravens always have wedge-shaped or at least very rounded tails, while a crow's tail is square. Another way to tell them apart is bill size (a raven's is heftier), and the last is by sound: ravens croak, gargle, bill-snap, and go *kok-kok-kruccck-kok,* while crows cry *caw, caw*—as we know from too many bad movies.

As a combo hatchet/crowbar, the raven's bill can pry open a dead deer or unlatch an ice chest. From roadkill to crawdads, if it crawls, wiggles, hops, or attracts maggots, the raven will have a go at it. A dumpster's pizza boxes or a dead seal are all the same to this guy. When the wolves come back to California (and they *will* come back), ravens will be ready to help do KP at the kill zone.

Ravens cache food for winter and have complex social organizations. In nighttime roosts they mutter and sigh, restless as a ward of insomniacs. They also hold a grudge: ravens that have been trapped for research studies quickly learn which cars go with which person, and while they'll ignore regular folks, they light off for the territories if a nemesis car rolls up.

In literature, ravens get to be the bad boys. It's the Trickster in some Native American traditions, sleeping with all the wives and stealing anything what ain't nailed down, and in stories from northern Europe, ravens hang with Odin, spying and ill-omening and being general henchmen. Yet their plumage shines with subtle beauty in the sun, and it's hard to fault an animal so much like us: curious, enduring, and seemingly oblivious to the carnage around us.

Real beauty is so deep you have to move into darkness to understand it.—Barry Lopez

How to Tell a Crow from a Raven

To make this pair easier to learn, here's a side-by-side comparison. Listen for the voice as well (*caw caw* versus croaks, knocks, and gargles), and consider habitat (crows spend more time in towns; ravens hang out more in mountains and deserts).

Crows are always sleeker, slimmer-billed, more urban.

Ravens are heavier and shaggier, with stouter bills.

Crows in flight show a squared (or slightly rounded) tail.

Ravens in flight show a diamond-shaped (or clearly rounded) tail.

Tree Swallow *Tachycineta bicolor*

👓 meadows, marshes, lakes, fields

> *True hope is swift, and flies with swallow's wings.*
> —William Shakespeare

Gleaming white below and midnight-blue above, tree swallows take "snappy dresser" to a new level. The name comes from holes-in-trees nesting choices, and they will use natural snags, old woodpecker holes, or human-supplied nest boxes (including ones intended for bluebirds). Tree swallows most often hunt over ponds, lakes, and marshes; between flights they perch on waterside branches to rest. Besides insects—and this is unique among this group—tree swallows also eat berries, which is one reason they can overwinter in California more often than other swallows.

Usually it's not a tricky bird to identify. The blue-white mix is easy to see and reliable as a field mark, so long as you check the rump. A violet-green swallow is almost the same color (especially in dull light) but has a white rump patch, not a solid back and tail the way a tree swallow does. Violet-greens are the higher-altitude species; one easy place to see violet-green swallows is around the tufa spires at Mono Lake. Tree swallows are more expected in the coastal lowlands, especially in winter. Only midsummer's newly fledged tree swallows are an exception. For the first summer they are still white underneath but mostly brown above, making them look like two birds not in this book: northern rough-winged swallows and bank swallows. That brown phase doesn't last long, and soon they molt into adult colors. Seen in good light, a tree swallow is not just lowercase blue, but an iridescent BLUE!

Do they hibernate in the bottoms of ponds? That was an English folk belief to explain where swallows go in winter, before migration had been figured out. Now we know that they shift to the tropics, though tree swallows are still moving south as late as November and December, and then barely get to the wintering sites before at least some are headed back north. Spring arrives early for this species; tree swallow migration begins as early as late January.

Cliff Swallow   *Petrochelidon pyrrhonota*

👀 cliffs, freeways, bridges, lakes, fields

You've almost certainly seen this one before, even if it's not yet on your list: other names could be culvert swallow, underside-of-bridge swallow, or even eaves-of-the-market-near-Lee-Vining-on-the-road-to-Yosemite swallow. Nesting in hectic colonies, it can be seen up and down I-5, on college campuses, along the California Aqueduct, and even, in small numbers, at Mission San Juan Capistrano, the famous home base for saintly birds.

It shares the usual swallow template for shape and behavior, and like other swallows it zooms and loops and power-dives as it scoops up insects. Tucked under overhangs or high-up corners, nests look like upside-down moonshine jugs and are built layer by layer out of tiny pellets of mud. Nests are jammed up side by side or even stacked on top of each other in dense swallow condominiums. That congenial togetherness helps identify this species; barn swallows don't pack together like this, and tree swallows prefer tree holes or nest boxes.

What color is a cliff swallow? Blue above, tan below, yet other colors mix in as well. A chestnut rump patch is one identification checkmark, and a miner's headlamp of bright ivory adds an accent to the blue heads and chestnut throats. The tail is short, squared off, and matter-of-fact: no barn swallow tail streamers here, and not even the tree swallow's shallow V. A look-alike species called the cave swallow nests in the main cave entrance at Carlsbad Caverns and also in limestone sinkholes in the Yucatán. It wanders to California about once a decade. Cliff, cave, and (some) tree swallows migrate to South America for the winter, returning as some of our earliest spring birds. Perhaps they all agree with Dorothy: there's no place like home.

When I rise up
let me rise up joyful
like a bird.

When I fall
let me fall without regret
like a leaf.

—Wendell Berry

Barn Swallow   *Hirundo rustica*

🔭 fields, meadows, beaches, marshes

The tail tells all: this might be better named the American fork-tailed swallow, since the deep V of the adult tail extends out on each side with an elegant swoosh. In accelerating flight the two sides can merge into a unified needle tail, and in younger birds the V is present but reduced. Both sexes contrast cobalt topsides with cinnamon face and tummy. (Juveniles are paler below.)

This is a common bird around the world. For us, it's a summer visitor, from late March to early October. By fall most North American barn swallows are heading south to Mexico and South America, though a few try out staycations and can be found in Southern California even in midwinter. It is an open-country feeder and can be seen over meadows, ponds, beaches, or fields—always with a zip and glide as graceful as skateboarders curling up a half-pipe.

The nest is as an adobe saucer of mud and straw, built under bridges, tucked in garage eaves, or hidden in the niche of a cliff. While it would be fun to log your first barn swallow next to an old barn (maybe with a barn owl inside), they also like beaches and tide pools, and in that habitat they often will be the only swallow species present. Look for beaches that still offer collisions of driftwood, pyramids of kelp, and slicks of low-tide sea lettuce, since a variety of layers means a variety of insects for barn swallows and black phoebes and sanderlings to chase and snatch. Beach-cruising swallows often course at eye level or lower, skimming right over the sand at jet-fighter speed, then banking and looping for a return pass.

Among sailors, barn swallow tattoos imply safe returns, and in literature this species was cited by Virgil, Shakespeare, and T. S. Eliot. Glass-half-empty people will say, *One swallow doesn't make a summer,* but optimists counter by noting that even one swallow provides us a day graced by unexpected joy.

> *At some point in life, the world's beauty becomes enough.*
> —Toni Morrison

How do you build a nest? One muddy twig at a time.

Mountain Chickadee *Poecile gambeli*

👀 pines (usually in mountains, sometimes lower)

The poet Mark Doty calls chickadees a "collectivity of sparks." Dancing and flitting through the pine forest, they hang upside down like bushtits but also, like juncos, come to feeders and, like nuthatches, spend time on branches and trunks. They are mostly after insects but they also like pine nuts, especially in winter, and will cache them as well. If the woods go bust, something called eruptive migration happens—basically you get a mess of chickadees flooding the lowlands, looking for replacement trees. They may find them; we have a *lot* of planted conifers in our cities. In lean times a mountain versus a well-forested backyard is not a distinction they can worry over, and in fall some might even turn up in the city parks of desert towns.

Mountain chickadees pair for life and are territorial about their nests, even attacking biologists who get too close. Mom may only be five inches long, but she's packing heat. Females can hiss like a snake to try to scare off things that are getting too close. Found throughout the American West, they center their interests on pines and pine relatives—spruces, firs, and piñon-juniper woodlands. A flock of chickadees and warblers sends out a lot of tittering contact calls, often heard by birders before the actual birds pass into view. Their usual song is a whistled version of their name, *chik-eh-deee-dah-deee*.

We have an inherent ability to see wild things, even if we're a bit rusty, our eyes not so sharp. Take children hiking and when they see a rabbit, a deer, a robin, a chickadee, you hear it in their voices, that excitement—"I see it, I see it!" Their voices are our voices: who doesn't want to be the first person on the hike to spot the big prize? If you're in the right mood, a mountain chickadee, black and white and nimble, is as good a prize as an eagle or a swan.

One touch of nature makes the whole world kin.—William Shakespeare

Chestnut-backed Chickadee *Poecile rufescens*

👀 coastal forests, northern mountains

The half-joking, half-wistful proposals to split California into two states, supposedly making it easier to govern, all need to propose an arbitrary midpoint. Perhaps the dividing line could be drawn using the range map of the chestnut-backed chickadee, since it's very much a top-half species. We start to see them in Cambria, mostly in wet, dense coastal forests, and by the time we reach Monterey, they're definitely part of the landscape. This species overlaps with mountain chickadees in the northern Sierra, nesting in self-excavated holes in rotten limbs (or in human-supplied nest boxes) with a preference for Douglas fir forests. Color changes with latitude: north of the Golden Gate, they show more chestnut along the flanks than they do when living farther south. From Marin County they carry on up to the wet Pacific Northwest and Alaska. They don't venture as far south as L.A. or San Diego, but there is one record of a solo bird that wintered in Santa Barbara and must not have liked it, because it never came back.

Like other chickadees, the chestnut-backed investigates the tips of branches, looking for insects or seeds, dangling, hovering, flitting, probing, and gleaning, often with a mixed flock of kinglets and warblers, all staying dialed in with a chatter of chips and *tseep*s.

It may be the ideal Independence Day hike someday: a walk through a coastal redwood forest, ferns everywhere, red trillium in bloom, and overhead, red as the redwood bark itself, the flitting, dancing forms of the chestnut-backed chickadee, aka the state bird of Jefferson, newest member of the United States of Cascadia.

Look and linger; don't just glance and go.
—Todd Newberry

Verdin and Bushtit
Auriparus flaviceps and *Psaltriparus minimus*

👓 desert scrub (verdins), forests and brush (bushtits)

Small and smaller this pair, and they are included together not for habitat—they don't often overlap—but for size and busyness. Less than three inches long, a bushtit weighs about the same as a teaspoon of sugar; the verdin, a skosh larger, sometimes weighs as much as two tips of the sugar spoon. Both are teeny, active birds, with chatterbox flocks flowing through branches or desert scrub like overexcited trick-or-treaters who have had too much candy. "This branch!—no, this one!—oh wait, here's one over here"—sometimes passing through the neighborhood before you ever had a chance for a decent look.

To be better at description, we have to work at attentiveness.—Mark Doty

Of the two, verdins are easier to identify and harder to find, since they're strictly desert birds. Live in Borrego Springs or Palm Desert? Dandy. You're sure to encounter these yellow-headed, gray-bodied fluffballs. Like the cactus wren, when not nesting they use nest balls for roosting, in order to conserve heat during cold winter nights. Palo verdes, smoke trees, creosote, mesquite: the bushes and trees of desert washes attract them most, as the birds check every shrub and branch for spiders and other juicy insects.

Acrobatically hanging upside down from the slimmest of branches and catkins, bushtits also are on extreme spider patrol, sometimes mingling with chickadees and warblers, sometimes hunting on their own. Males have dark eyes; females, yellow. Broadly speaking, bushtits can be found more or less everywhere, including in backyards, gardens, parks, chaparral, oak woodlands, and weedy fields. You can find them in Exposition Park in downtown Los Angeles, on Santa Cruz Island, or on campus at UC Berkeley. Bushtits have a whispery, chittering way of keeping in touch, and it seems almost as if they sift through the forest, light as willow dander.

Verdins (top and bottom left) and bushtits (top and bottom right).

White-breasted Nuthatch *Sitta carolinensis*

🔭 pines (usually in mountains, sometimes lower)

White-breasted nuthatches don't just live in trees, they live *on* trees, inching up and down tree trunks, chasing spiders, and chivvying out beetles. Brown creepers do that too, but creepers climb from the ground up, the expected way, while nuthatches go down trees headfirst. (Doesn't all the blood rush to their heads?) They also can hitch sideways and they will follow the main branches out away from the trunk surprisingly far, as often hanging from the bottom as walking on top. It's as if in their minds they live on a zero-gravity planet and can't understand why the rest of us, boring lumps of mud that we are, don't follow them in their exploration of the underside of everything.

White-breasted nuthatches make ID easy: dark cap, white face, gray back, sharp bill, tree-hugger habits. In California, there are two overlapping possibilities besides our main choice. Smaller and more forest-loving than the white-breasted kind, red-breasted nuthatches have a line through the eye and sport red bellies. In the Sierra, they stick mostly to conifers and they have an *eenk eenk* squeeze-horn call. In contrast, white-breasted nuthatches are either lower down the mountain in the oaks or above the pines in the alpine zone, leaving the spruce and fir trees to their red-breasted relations. Smaller and browner than either of these, pygmy nuthatches can skitter right out to the very tips of branches and cones, finding the spiders and seeds that the other two nuthatches can't reach.

How many types of white-breasted nuthatches are there in the world? For now just one species, but populations with different calls and different genetics and habitats imply that if we look closely, there may be another species or two or three that we just have not parsed yet. Science is not an all-seeing, all-knowing omnipotence but rather a series of claims and rebuttals, insights and retractions, and ornithology remains a young field, one filled with unanswered questions.

Pygmy nuthatch (below)—
small bird, big ambitions.

Brown Creeper *Certhia americana*

This one comes to you, rather than you going to it—or more exactly, you can go to the woods, then once there, just wait to see what turns up. Creepers don't often flock, and they're brown as the trees they crawl on, spiraling up the trunk to get all the spiders and beetles in each and every crack in the bark. That can make them tricky to learn how to find, but they are more common than you might guess, and they often share small, sharp, very high-pitched *zzeet zzeet* contact calls, which can make them easier to track down.

Small as the brown creeper is—almost like a stealthy mouse with a piece of bark tied to its back—it prefers the biggest trees, including coastal redwoods, Douglas firs, and the sugar pines and incense cedars of the High Sierra. That means you find them in vacation spots like Yosemite and Big Sur, and in wet urban forests, including the trees of Golden Gate Park. Yet L.A. and Fresno can have them in the foothill parks (especially in winter), Angeles Crest has good numbers, and in San Diego, brown creepers make it as far south as the Laguna Mountains.

The brown creeper would make a good addition to fairy stories, since it nests behind loose bark in a hammock made from very fine vegetation. Unlike nuthatches (which often go *down* the tree, headfirst), creepers feed by scooching *up* a tree, propped up by their stiff tails like shrink-rayed woodpeckers. At the top (with sometimes a few side trips first along the bigger branches), they flit down to the base of the next tree over, and the spider-hunting spiral begins all over again.

We're so big! First just let the habitat recover from the shock of your arrival.
—Todd Newberry

Marsh Wren *Cistothorus palustris*

marshes, reedy lakeshores

Meet Thumbelina after four espressos. Up and down its empire of cattails, the marsh wren rattles, scolds, and fusses, in view for the briefest click of your fingers and then off elsewhere to snatch an insect or chase a rival out of its no-fly zone. Males can produce up to two hundred songs (mostly raspy trills, but still, that's a lot). Ever vigilant, they even sing in the middle of the night.

Always and only found in and around marshes, these wrens inhabit bulrushes and reeds in fresh, brackish, or salt water. In California they don't need to migrate far, other than maybe downslope or down the road a little, and they are supplemented with birds coming in from farther north. The male takes courting 'n' sparking seriously: to be sure he attracts the right lady, he builds a circuit of ten or twelve demonstration nests, then invites her for a tour. Do they use them all? Some may be night roosts, some may be places to stash fledglings, some may be decoys to evade predators, or some (or all) may be useless follies just created so he can demonstrate his domestic prowess. Maybe that should be a question on a dating form for humans: *How fast can you build a plywood shed?* You can never have enough storage space.

This is a distinctly small bird. How small? Pretty darn small. A really top-of-its-weight-class marsh wren, perhaps even ready for a New Year's resolution and a fitness membership, it still weighs less than three grapes.

*The reeds give
way to the*

*wind and give
the wind away*

—A. R. Ammons

Sunrise over cattails—
welcome to the marsh
wrens' empire.

Bewick's Wren   *Thryomanes bewickii*

👀 oak woodlands, brushy yards, stream edges

With cocked tails and a can-do attitude, wrens fearlessly take on the world, flitting and darting, scolding and fussing, and stopping only long enough to pour out one of a dozen trilling songs. Bewick's wrens hunt spiders up and down branches and underneath leaves, mostly in oak forests and chaparral but also down to the edge of the desert, along streams, and in bushy parks, gardens, and well-watered backyards.

Especially during breeding season, male Bewick's wrens tee up on the tops of bushes and trees and really belt it out. The capacity to sing is innate; the young bird learns the particular melodies and riffs from males on surrounding territories. His total set list may include twenty songs, which is either charming or frustrating, depending on your point of view. As you're gaining experience in birding by ear, wrens may send you chasing into the bushes many times in a row.

As is usual in California, several options exist besides the default species. A wren in cattails is almost always a marsh wren; a Bewick's wren with a shorter tail and no eyestripe is a house wren. If you're in Muir Woods or some other cathedral of moss and dim light, watch low down for the Pacific wren (called winter wren in older books), which is even smaller and shorter-tailed—a microbot version of an already wee beast.

Thomas Bewick was a British engraver (and contemporary of William Blake) whose work John James Audubon admired; his name is pronounced like the car, Buick. Mr. Bewick never met this New World species in person, but if he had, he probably would have called it a jenny wren and would have known a folk jig or two featuring it, including this one: "The wren was so cute and we were so cunning, / He hid in the bush while we were out running."

The house wren (right), another woodland bird, is smaller and plainer than a Bewick's.

Canyon wrens (left) especially like verticality: cliffs, narrow canyons, and scree slopes. Where forests and canyons combine, they overlap with Bewick's wrens.

Cactus Wren   *Campylorhynchus brunneicapillus*

👀 Joshua tree woodlands, low deserts, coastal sage

Most wrens are small and brown, with cocked tails and a woodland lifestyle. The largest wren in North America, the cactus wren, changes *Skills start as habits. At first, just be willing to look or listen.—Simon Barnes* that up. It is both a desert bird and, in lingering but important populations, also part of the coastal sage community, a botanical assemblage that is native to places like San Diego or the Palos Verdes Peninsula, right where a lot of expensive houses want to be built.

Boldly patterned with a large white eyestripe, speckled breast, and a long, banded tail, Arizona's state bird nests right in the heart of a thorny bush or even a cholla cactus. The nest, which is also used as a night roost, is a ball of grass. Cactus wrens come into yards in desert towns but are generally birds of the open desert or coastal scrub, finding their insect prey on the ground and also nabbing lizards or eggs from small birds like verdins. In listing what they eat at feeders, one book mentions apple slices and fried potatoes, which probably tells us more about homeowners and their leftovers than it does about the wren's actual dietary preferences.

The song is distinctive. Ornithologist Kimball Garrett says this species deserves the Oscar for most ubiquitous birdsong on movie sound tracks, but it might be a three-way tie between it, the California quail, and the American crow. The cactus wren song is raspy and accelerating, transcribed as a *cha-cha-cha* or a quickly repeated *chug, chug-chug, chug chug chug chug,* like a car engine finally cranking over. You even will hear it in science fiction movies.

Why Do Birds Sing?

Birds sing after a storm. Why shouldn't we?—Rose Kennedy

Lions roar and crickets chirp, but only birds sing, at least in terms of ranges humans can hear. (Humpback whales sing, but not to us.) Genus *Homo* probably has been in love with bird sounds for many tens of thousands of years. Poets write odes to nightingales, territorial warblers tell us spring is here, and no movie sound track would be complete without bird sounds to foreshadow doom or verify that we're in the "woods" and not a Hollywood backlot.

Birds sing using a mix of innate and learned behavior. None of us can sing like a bird because birds use a special organ called a syrinx. This resembles our vocal cords but is longer, stronger, and divided in two branches, so some birds can make two kinds of sound at once. Types of birdsong define territories—"Keep out! This seat is taken!"—and attract mates both by advertising presence ("I'm here!") and also by implying fitness or dominance ("Hey ladies, check out the stereo speakers on *this* lowrider!"). Duetting may reinforce pair bonding. Location matters: because of the background noise, birds in the city have to sing louder than forest birds.

More generally, bird sounds help flocks stay in touch, sound the alarm if Neighborhood Watch reports an owl (see "Mobbing," page 136), help parents find chicks in crowded colonies, allow chicks to remind Dad that they're hungry, or even serve as echolocation. A cave-roosting night bird called the oilbird (distantly related to the whip-poor-will), gives off a series of audible clicks, just as a bat does, to navigate in the dark.

None of these explanations includes terms like "exuberance" or "happiness." While logic trains us to tut-tut such nonsense, listen to a wren or warbler and a word like "joy" soon rises to the top of the list—if not theirs, then at least ours.

Fluffed up on a cold morning, this yellow-rumped warbler will soon start moving through the treetops to feed. It will stay in contact with flockmates by giving a bright chip note, audible even when the bird isn't in view.

Wrens (like this house wren) are dinky, round-bodied birds with short tails. Usually found on their own, they can be low in the tree or high. Their voices are always larger than their bodies.

American Dipper   *Cinclus mexicanus*

The dipper is not a shorebird but lives its life in, on, by, and under water. Most of us enjoy this plump, slate-gray bird when we are in Yosemite near the Happy Isles Bridge, or downstream behind the town of El Portal. Yet it can be found throughout the Sierra, in the north coast's wet forests, and down into the mountains of Southern California. John Muir famously loved it, using the older name of water ouzel and calling it the darling of streams and the hummingbird of blooming water.

A dipper hunts in rivers and mountain streams alone, as casually at ease below the water as above it. On midstream rocks it blinks white eyelids and bobs urgently up and down, as if bursting to share the right answer with the teacher. Underwater it becomes an old-fashioned diver in an invisible brass helmet, walking along the bottom, poised to uncover doubloons and shipwrecks (or at least beetles and fish eggs). The poor thing will never be America's top model, not with that stubby beak, those short legs, and that abbreviated tail. Yet it can fly underwater (swimming with its wings) and see underwater too (thanks to special eyelids), and its prolific oil glands keep its feathers extra waterproof.

Dippers need fast, clean streams, so their presence indicates good water quality. Sometimes trout or hawks try to eat them, but mostly they have to think about the weather. They are willing to hold their home territory into winter, lasting in the high country even as snow piles up—just so long as their creeks do not freeze completely. (In that case, they just migrate downstream a bit.) As John Muir said, praising the dipper's music, "Both in winter and summer he sings, sweetly, cheerily, independent alike of sunshine and of love, requiring no other inspiration than the stream on which he dwells. While water sings, so must he."

To put your hands in a river is to feel the chords that
bind the earth together.—Barry Lopez

Western Bluebird *Sialia mexicana*

👀 open forests, fields, meadows, parks

A forest and glade bird, oak and grassland too, the bluebird scans for fly-by insects, dashing out from post and branch. Alternately, seeing something suitable on the ground, it might hover first before pouncing. Males dress to impress, and as Thoreau says, "the bluebird carries the sky on his back." How best to describe the color? It's too dark to be cornflower blue, yet richer, more saturated than federal blue. Is it ultramarine? Maybe Yves Klein blue matches best. The bluebird differs from the flycatchers because it's actually a small thrush, and as such it flocks more often and also feeds on berries, especially in winter.

Female bluebirds are gray with a blue rinse; first-summer juveniles are checkered with black-edged spots. Winter sends the family into the lowlands; summer birds are expected in ponderosa pines or other open, meadowy forests. They nest in holes, either dug out by woodpeckers or provided by nest boxes. Pastures, even city parks work: the bluebird needs trees but also open ground, and is associated with borders and edges where brush and trees meet open ground. Selective logging and small wildfires provide standing deadwood for nest holes, and clearings in which to hunt—nature is never static, and some species need at least local, small-scale fires to provide a mosaic of habitats. (Scientists in making this observation are not speaking about the fifty-mile-wide, unstoppable conflagrations that burn up an entire mountain range.)

Another kind of bluebird overlaps with this one in California; it lives higher in the mountains in summer and disperses into deserts in winter. This kind, the mountain bluebird, is pale blue underneath (never chestnut), while an eastern bluebird (like the western one, also blue and chestnut) does not occur in California.

Paradise is our native country, and we in this world be as exiles and strangers.
—*Richard Greenham*

American Robin *Turdus migratorius*

👓 woodlands, forest edges, yards, parks

Three cheers to the robin for being easy to see and even easier to identify. As American as Barbie, deep-fried Twinkies, and zombie movies, robin redbreast is a forest bird that retired to the suburbs. With its potbellied profile and cheerful spring whistles, it is common and well known, staying in most habitats year-round. Robins love city parks and big lawns but also do fine in forests, meadows, orchards, gardens, and all but the most austere deserts. (And even there, one might turn up in migration.)

Both sexes have cinnamon-red tummies; eye crescents and a sturdy orange bill complete the package. Our other California thrushes are usually brown-backed and spot-chested or, in the case of varied thrush, striped orange and blue. The robin wears color proudly and can be identified even halfway across the park. Only fresh-from-the-nest juveniles are streaky-blotchy in perplexing ways, but even those have an underpainting of red across the chest beneath the streaks, and they turn all-red as summer turns to fall.

Berries top the menu in fall and winter; worms and insects add to the list in summer, with snails and lizards as chance allows. The hunter was once the hunted: in the soup-pot days of pioneer settlement, robins were shot and eaten in large numbers. (We forget, often, how much wild game was hanging in the windows of most butcher shops.) Nests can be low or high but typically will be about ten feet up in the crotch of a shady tree. Robins require mud to finish off the nest.

In Europe "robin" refers to a red-breasted flycatcher smaller than a black phoebe; nearsighted or just inaccurate, the Pilgrims applied the term to our robust, ground-loving thrush. Storms sometimes blow the odd stray to Europe; in French the name is *merle d'Amérique,* which sounds like a brand of fancy cologne, and in the UK the arrival of an American robin can cause a traffic jam of twitchers (as hard-core British listers are called). Here, where robins form winter flocks, we almost start to take them for granted—but shouldn't.

It really *is* true—the early bird gets the worm (left).

Varied Thrush *Ixoreus naevius*

👀 wet, cool forests and wet, cool parks

This slate-blue robin knows how to spin a color wheel. What complements dark blue? Burnt orange, of course, which it has on wing bars, throat, and again the chest, just in case you missed it. The final result is surprising yet oddly perfect.

This is one of our groundlings; it forages in low bushes and so is not to be expected up in the highest crown of the tree with the warblers and kinglets. To feed, varied thrushes scuffle among leaf litter, hopping, scratching, tugging, and turning, unless they've found a bush bursting with ripe berries, in which case they may gorge side by side with American robins.

The usual call is an ethereal whistle. Learning to track birds by ear is its own special pleasure (or frustration), sometimes easier for younger folks than older, and easier perhaps for those who have not endured a lot of gunfire, freeway roar, or heavy metal concerts. Calling or silent, the varied thrush is an old-growth, big-tree sort of bird, and it loves wet shade, whether in Alaska and the Pacific Northwest, where it breeds, or in wintering spots like Muir Woods or the Pacific Grove cemetery. Populations rise and fall every other year; some winters it visits the southern half of the state too, and in "flight years" one might find it in fall in desert oases or even as far south as the date palms of the Salton Sea. For the most part, expect it in dim light and wet forests, mostly north of the Golden Gate Bridge.

Who can make a delicate adventure
Of walking on the ground?
                    —*Maxwell Bodenheim*

California Thrasher   *Toxostoma redivivum*

👀 chaparral, brushy parks, stream edges

Even if you're new to birdwatching, many of the birds already are familiar: you probably know the jay and crow and sparrow. And then there's this guy—a gleaner of the understory leaf litter that looks some mad scientist's cross between a towhee and a curlew. Seeing your first thrasher can make you turn your head a bit sideways and think, "What the heck?"

California thrashers live in brushland chaparral, and less so along streams and the bushy edges of gardens and parks. They sing in the open but forage by raking the shadows for insects, seeds, and fruit. Expect them along the coast and foothills, with a range that matches their California name (including some of northern Baja). The thrasher isn't really a forest or high-altitude bird, and it doesn't migrate or wander around much. Once you learn to recognize the profile, you can identify it even if it's backlit at dawn. The thrasher is common but hard to predict, and to see one, the best thing is just to hike a lot—a good idea in general, even if you don't want to add a new bird to your life list.

The common name combines the Old English words for thrush with the words for threshing grain. (*Thrasher* is also a skateboard magazine.) In the sagebrush of the Owens Valley, a shorter-billed, more mockingbird-y species can be found—the sage thrasher—and in sandy washes of the Mojave Desert scurries the LeConte's thrasher. The LeConte's looks like the California thrasher but is paler and takes over the creosote lowlands once that rival species leaves off. Tamarisk thickets at the Salton Sea add the crissal thrasher, with pale eyes and a maroon, not tan, undertail.

Movie stars and thrashers both love living in the Hollywood Hills.

Northern Mockingbird *Mimus polyglottos*

👓 yards, parks, woodland edges, suburbia

Gray body, long tail, white wing flashes in flight: must be a mockingbird. Slim but active, and thanks to the wings usually easy to spot in flight, this will probably be one of your first IDs as you begin to learn the names of common birds.

Atticus Finch in *To Kill a Mockingbird* says not to harm these guys, since they don't eat crops and they sing for our pleasure. That's only half true. While they eat insects and berries, not food crops, their many-voiced song is a good example of what Darwin meant by "sexual selection." The song has nothing to do with our pleasure or even theirs (except for the cigarettes-in-bed phase, afterward): the male attracts a mate through the vigor and complexity of his song. Indeed, the Latin name means "many tongued," and males can sing day and night, year-round, though females sing as well, and there are many lesser sounds, including a *chakk* note and a sort of scolding chatter. If somebody is singing outside your window in the middle of the night and it's not Romeo, blame this guy. As they try to outdo one another, male mockingbirds will co-opt a variety of songs and noises, even car alarms, mastering up to two hundred different phrases.

This is more a bird of town and deserts and woodland edges than the high mountains, and it has adapted well to life in the leafy suburbs. Any park or residential block will probably have one. Watch for them on the tops of trees and phone poles or even hopping across the lawn, chasing things down like the diminutive T. rex that it is. Mockingbirds live here year-round and also nest on the Channel Islands and in Mexico.

The bugs are always greener on the other side the closed area (above).

European Starling *Sturnus vulgaris*

👓 cities, yards, parks, fields, orchards

European starlings came to America in the 1890s, released by a well-intentioned but badly misguided Shakespeare appreciation society. Now they number 200 million just in North America alone. It would have been better if the Bard's fans had given out copies of the plays or recited sonnets on street corners: the starling's rap sheet includes raiding crops, creating a rain of poo below winter roosts, and driving native birds out of nest holes.

Late one afternoon in October
I hear them for the first time:
loud-voiced palavering, whistles,
* murmurs,*
quarrels, bickering and warbling,
* croaking and chatter*
in the high plane trees of the street.
*   —Jesper Svenbro*

Starlings look glossy year-round and in fall add white speckles on top of the purply-greeny-blackish base coat. This star-spangled plumage changes as the breeding season approaches and the sparkling feather tips wear off. The bill (yellowest in spring) is long, sharp, and multipurpose; starlings fossick for waste grain, hunt insects, raid orchards, probe lawns, and glean seeds from weedy lots.

Stout-bodied and short-winged, starlings in flight look like magical lumps of coal: how *do* they stay in the air? Yet fly they do, and often with balletic precision. A winter flock of thousands and thousands of starlings swirling in unison is called a murmuration; this behavior is seen more often in agricultural areas than mid-city, and more often on viral videos than in daily experience. Still, it's a real thing. There's no mind control, just ultra-fast responses, as each bird cues off of its seven nearest neighbors, who in turn are responding to their neighbors, on through the flock. The result is a black cloud of birds twisting and swirling in unison. (Off camera, there's probably a peregrine falcon or Cooper's hawk setting off the stampede.)

Wherever you live, starlings are probably abundant and near at hand. In mainland Europe there has been a decline in starling populations, but most ornithologists in the U.S.A. would say, "Oh, that's okay, here, have some of ours."

Winter's breast spots (left) wear smooth in spring (right).

Cedar Waxwing *Bombycilla cedrorum*

parks, yards, and forests with berry-filled plants

Waxwings follow the berries and can be found in backyards, parks, gardens, farms, orchards and desert oases—places with mistletoe, toyon, crab apple, Peruvian pepper, Russian olive, or any other tree or bush that brims with berries and fruits. Introduced plant or native species, somebody's yard or the side of a mountain, it's all the same to them. When they will come, when they will leave, that part nobody can predict, other than that midsummer is least likely, and so fall and winter are more expected. Once on the job, *zeee zeee*, the flock buzzes to one another, staying in touch as they harvest every berry on the tree. When done, up they lift and off they go, as a compact, synchronized mass, leaving as suddenly as they arrived.

Three field marks help us name it for what it is. The first is the head: the peaked crest is well-combed but not confrontational, and the black eye mask is made for beauty contests not banditry. The second is the velvety, silky look to the body itself. Compact and well-ranged, the body somehow looks tidy and luxurious, never ratty or disheveled. The third ties in with the name, since the bottom edge of the folded wing has glossy red teardrops, like splatters of old-fashioned sealing wax. (What do they do? Nobody knows.) The cedar waxwing is the cedar waxwing because of the total suite of actions and behaviors—the contact call, the companionable group feeding, the eager, nearly frantic investigation of the tree's full fruit crop. Adding these features together always equals this species.

A waxwing gorging on berries encourages reforestation. It will digest the pulp but void the seeds, making this species a great pal to trees. Waxwings not only help redistribute the seeds to neighboring districts (rather than letting them mound up under the parent tree, as gravity does), but each time they eat a berry and pass the pit or stone, they wrap the outgoing pip in a nourishing layer of fertilizer, also known as bird poo. If you're a plant, you can't ask for a better start in life than that.

Cedar waxwings are sleek and handsome, usually found in flocks in berry trees.

Northern Red Bishop *Euplectes franciscanus*
Scaly-breasted Munia *Lonchura punctulata*

👀 weedy, marshy fields (small populations, yet spreading)

These are both new to American bird books: the bishop is an African marsh finch about the size of a house sparrow, and the munia (or mannikin) is an escaped cage bird native to Asia. One pet trade name for it is the spice finch. Just as with Southern California's parrots, they only live here because somebody left the window open. Still, it seems to be working out, and in San Diego, Orange, and Los Angeles Counties, munias are so well-established that the national rule-makers allow them to be counted on North American life lists. Besides the core urban range, they've also got outposts in Riverside, San Bernardino, Ventura, and Santa Barbara Counties, and if you miss them there, Houston has some too. (And Hawai'i and Australia, and and and…)

Chestnut red with a chain mail black-and-white chest, munias really love tall, weedy, unmowed grass (what Shakespeare would have called "rank vegetation") such as you find on sandbars and in rivers, around marshy ponds, and in overgrown recharge basins. Willows and tall, brushy nearby cover will add to the "ahh, just right" effect for them.

At first glance bishops look like vermilion flycatchers but are chubbier, black-bellied, and have a wide, seed-cracking bill. If in display mode, they stand out from a long way away, but part of the year they're in the avian version of sweats and old T-shirt, just streaky brown and tan, and so can be easy to overlook. In Southern California they match most munia locations, and in South San Francisco Bay, bishop records come from the Shoreline and Sunnyvale waterfronts and scattered inland sites. Santa Cruz reports them as well.

What long-term harm they will or won't cause, how far they will or won't spread, nobody can yet predict. Have a Ouija board? Time to try it out. For now, they are here (for better or worse), and at least they are very handsome beasts.

When in doubt, wear red.
—Bill Blass

Munias (above) harvest grass seeds. A red bishop (left) displays full color.

House Sparrow   *Passer domesticus*

everywhere we are

In 1851 America was so new the paint wasn't even dry. The Civil War was ten long years away; transcontinental railroads more distant still. Abe Lincoln was a hayseed lawyer in Illinois. Rivers of passenger pigeons flowed through the skies, and buffalo carpeted the prairies. Yet in Brooklyn, a cage of brown-backed, black-bibbed weaver finches known as spuggies or chissicks was about to change America forever. Once released, there would be no going back. Simple math: 2 become 4 become 16, until 60 million house sparrows filled North America (with half a billion more worldwide).

It was brought here not for its song (which is a simple *cheep cheep*). The intent was that they would eat worms and other farm pests; except most of the year sparrows gobble down seeds—either picked out of horse droppings (fine) or stolen from the crops themselves (uh-oh). They began nesting in and around barns and farms, and those are still their favorite spots, but they'll also go for stoplights, neon signs, drainage holes, old trees, bluebird nest boxes, and about a thousand other nooks, crannies, cavities, and protected eaves. (They will even take over cliff swallow nests.) To raise young they need protein in the form of bugs and worms, but otherwise they'll gladly come to backyard feeders, the spilled grain at rail yards, or weeds in lots so small and forgotten they're not even included on Google Maps. Everywhere they go, they muscle in on territory, making themselves at home.

Males are gray-cheeked, brown-capped, and black-bibbed, with a stout, conical, seed-cracking bill and a generally robust size (as sparrows go). Females have a tan racing stripe over the eye and a streaky back but they look like most other sparrows. The poet Gerald Stern, citing his mother's Yiddish, teasingly calls the sparrow "a bit of a schnorrer"—a bum, somebody who cadges handouts. We might be better to name him the ultimate survivor, and praise him as such. After all, if you had to bet on just one critter to last out the next thousand years, would you put your money on the panda, the peacock, or, down among the crumbs at our feet, the humble but durable house sparrow?

House Finch *Haemorhous mexicanus*

 parks, yards, woodland edges

House finches are streaky brown sparrows common in yards and towns, edges and vineyards, with stubby, seed-cracking bills and slim, V-notched tails. They love backyard feeders and any kind of grassy opening with hedges or trees nearby. Females look the same from one to the next, but males vary widely: some are a pale, washed-out pink, while others paint the town red. All sources agree that spring males pour out a cheerful, attractive song; trying to transcribe that song turns otherwise plain-speaking ornithologists into bad Victorian poets. It might make more sense if field guides just said about the song, "Try Googling it."

Why red? We're not quite sure. The rules of sexual selection suggest it's one of the symbols that causes one chap to be labeled prom king while his rival shuffles in the corner, staring at his shoes. House finches are a good model for illustrating sexual selection because males are red but variably so, and sometimes they're not red but yellow. We know for sure that females prefer more color-saturated mates. Since the red comes from carotenoid pigments in their food, are redder males visibly advertising better foraging skills or stronger immune systems? They are perhaps able to tolerate parasites better, or better resist disease. Or maybe all males forage equally well but the redder males just have some genetic predisposition that is manifested in redness, sort of like, "Everybody in my family lives to be a hundred, heck if I know why." The final answer awaits a future puzzle master.

There must have been a time when they had to rough it, making do with chaparral and meadows, but with the settlement of the West, they've become strongly associated with human-influenced habitats, and, having been introduced to the eastern U.S.A. in the 1940s, house finches are filling in the map from sea to shining sea. (They also have been present in Hawai'i since the 1870s.) If you want encouragement to switch to an all-veg diet, one bumper sticker might read, *Eat more sunflower seeds: a billion house finches can't be wrong.*

This page shows house finches. Purple finches (bottom left) and Cassin's finches (not shown) can be found in the mountains.

Lesser Goldfinch   *Spinus psaltria*

👀 weedy fields, woodland edges, parks, yards

Small and lively, lesser goldfinches usually like open places with lots of seeds—either from weedy plants or somebody's feeder, they don't care. They shuck seeds skillfully, shelling them rapid fire and spitting out the hulls. Ours in California are green-backed with a black cap; cross paths with this same species in Texas or South America and puzzle over the all-black back. Why don't they have that here? Nobody knows. Habits, though, remain the same: noisy flocks hang upside down from alders or sunflowers, or sing from cottonwoods, or make a wet, weedy edge of a park come alive with color. They love bird feeders, where they jockey with house finches, sparrows, chickadees, and juncos.

As a term, "lesser goldfinch" implies a small body, which is accurate, but there really are no "greater" goldfinches that this one would be "lesser" to. Birders sometimes call them lesters, and bird banders tally them in notebooks using the four-letter code LEGO. Each of those terms feels a bit un-right, yet both beat the previous folk name: tarweed canary.

Two other goldfinches are possible to see in California, and on average, American goldfinches are a bit easier to come by in Northern California. Males are yellow as yellow can be, with black-and-white wings and a perfect black hat. In the south, Lawrence's goldfinches belong more to the open-and-arid camp, sticking to chaparral and oaks and deserts. Black-faced and yellow-winged, they don't come to feeders as often, and it's hard to predict where you'll find them. Their motto is *You'll see me when you see me.* Some bird guides call the Lawrence's goldfinch "erratic" (which makes it sound moody and unreliable), while other books prefer a more romantic, Bedouins-on-camels evocation: "nomadic." Both terms mean that it has its own itinerary from year to year—a plan it's not interested in sharing with any of us.

My friend is adept at being among birds, making a quiet place inside her. One time, three goldfinches perched on a branch just above her, and she whispered, "Do you think they know how happy they are?"
—Charles Goodrich

Planting a yard for wildlife looks good, smells good, and the goldfinches will love you forever.

Pishing: How to Fish for Songbirds

When unknown things simmer in the middle of the bushes, flickering and darting, never showing themselves at all, some frustrated birders don't just stand there, they pish. This fussing or scolding noise is an attempt to imitate the sound of birds flocking around an intruder. One pishes in the hope that birds will pop into view, curious about what's going on. Is it a snake? An owl? What's up? While they come out in the open, you make a quick survey. Pishing usually doesn't make any difference, but you feel better trying, since at least you're doing *something*.

The easiest way to learn is by copying others, though there are also the inevitable YouTube videos. To try it yourself, wet your lips, then kiss the side of your hand while making an urgent and protracted shushing sound. Let the cadence rise and fall, mixing in some spluttering and scolding.

Harder to create but sometimes more effective, the tooting call of a northern pygmy owl can also trigger a confab of songbirds, all ready to band together to drive off the unwelcome predator. This sound does take some rehearsal and needs to be a fairly convincing impression to trigger results. You purse your mouth into a tight O and whistle on the exhaled breath, *tooot* (pause) *tooot* (pause) *tooot*. Sometimes nothing happens, and sometimes the real owl will turn up. You have nothing to lose in trying (except maybe your dignity).

Hearing vigorous pushing, a yellow warbler looks down and thinks, "Oh, it's only you."

Taking pictures at the zoo? Pishing can help perk up a bored or drowsy animal. This fishing cat, native to Southeast Asia, was photographed in San Diego.

Common Yellowthroat   *Geothlypis trichas*

marshes, reedy lakeshores, wet parks

When we hear a bird sing, life touches life.—Charles Hartshorne

Wichity witchity wichity sings the male yellowthroat, perched on a twig or stem of tule reed. The rest of the time he's down low, combing through cattails and willows anywhere there's marshy ground, including saltwater lagoons, streams, farm ponds, sloughs, and wet, bushy city parks. You can see the common yellowthroat at both ends of your vacation, with one in the morning along water's edge in Oakland, and a different subspecies waiting for you at Crane Flat when you pull into Yosemite to camp. While the mountain birds move to the lowlands for winter, along the coast the yellowthroat is year-round, as it is along the Colorado River.

Males and females both have yellow throats…usually. First-year birds can be drab enough to puzzle experts, but habitat (marshy ground, stream edges) and habits (low to the ground, tail cocked, *tsk-tsking,* hard to see well) add up to a pretty certain guess. Nests are woven by females out of grass; they are about three inches around and sometimes form a complete dome like a sedge igloo. Males wear bandit masks all year, and the male's four-part color pattern on the head is especially striking when they're singing in morning sunlight. Green cap, gray sweatband, black mask, and blazing yellow throat and chest—just fabulous. Designing a flag for a new country? Look how well these stripes of pure color play against each other.

Compact and busy, they eat spiders, moths, dragonflies, termites, and caterpillars, and they resemble wrens in their active, short-tailed profile. Yet they are bigger than brown-and-black marsh wrens and always more brightly colored, with at least some wash of green and a hint of muted yellow. With a bit of patience, brief glimpses finally become clear views as they pause in the open.

This intent fellow (right) looks like an extreme sports fan who has painted his face for the big game.

Yellow Warbler *Setophaga petechia*

 woodlands, foresty parks, stream edges

Warblers are quick and active, thin-billed, usually gorgeous of voice, and companionable of spirit, flickering through the tops of trees in mixed flocks.

Nature is not a place to visit. It is home.
—*Gary Snyder*

For many birdwatchers, *the* bird—the quintessential example of the order Aves—is a warbler. To those folks, nothing is more indelibly birdy than this group, and nothing better symbolizes spring's return in the American consciousness. Of course the affection is not without risks. "Warbler neck" refers to the crick one gets from peering up too long and too intently. (Hint: To take the weight off your neck, buy a shoulder harness for your binoculars.)

Yellow warblers pour through California in spring migration and breed in streamside trees and second growth, especially alders, willows, and cottonwoods. Short-tailed and plain-faced for a warbler, it might be more accurately called the yellow-with-thin-streaks-of-chestnut warbler. Fall birds are grayer but still have the black-eye-on-a-plain-face look of spring birds, and the same yellow (or yellowish, or at least not all-dark) tail. After breeding they'll disperse into pines and mixed forests, and in fall migration they can be found even in city parks.

This species suffers from brood parasitism, when one bird (in this case, the brown-headed cowbird) lays its eggs in another bird's nest. The intruder's eggs hatch first and the unwitting parent raises somebody else's babies, while the young of the "correct" species all perish. Cowbirds used to follow buffalo herds and could not stick around a nest. Moving often made their impact on the regular birds of a given area much lighter. Now that cowbirds are full-time residents (at stables and so forth), many yellow warbler populations are suffering. It is a classic case of "the knee bone is connected the ankle bone." Change one relationship (kill the buffalo; put cattle in permanent feedlots and horses in stables), and it has a knock-on effect on a dozen other relationships.

Wilson's warbler (left) is yellow but the males show an all-black cap.

Like other warblers, the yellow warbler (above) has a thin bill, a slim profile, and an active foraging style.

Yellow-rumped Warbler *Setophaga coronata*

 forests, streams, parks, yards

Common, widespread, and showing up in a variety of forms, yellow-rumps (lovingly still called butter butts) make life better every month of the year. In California, they are our main fall, winter, and spring warblers in the lowlands. In summer they breed in forests from the foothills to the alpine zone. Collectively, we have more individuals of this kind than we do of any other warbler species.

Males in spring have yellow splotches all over, like a toddler helping to paint a house. The head, the chin, under the arms, across the butt—these all are blazing yellow, filled in with gray, black, and limited amounts of white. Fall females are simplest and drabbest, being unpatterned grayish green. In all phases, a yellow rump patch sets off the tail from the back, and seeing that feature then stops any further guesswork. If it has the yellow on top of the butt, that makes it this kind of bird.

Yellow-rumped warblers like trees, but after that it's pretty much *Mi casa es su casa,* since they do yards and median plantings, actual mountain forests, desert oases, pocket parks, college campuses, jogging paths, and parking lots. Find some trees, maybe eventually some water, and yellow-rumped warblers do the rest.

In winter, locate a flock by listening for the sharp chip notes. Expect variety: there is an East Coast form of the yellow-rumped called the myrtle warbler (after the wax myrtle tree), and also the flock may be tangled up with chickadees and other warbler species, creating what bird books call a mixed feeding flock. The main California yellow-rumped form is called Audubon's warbler; it used to be a separate species (and to some birders still is), but there's a broad overlap range of hybrids. That interbreeding violates one of the oldest principles of what makes a species a species, so Audubon's and myrtle warblers were lumped together and given the current name.

That leaves some people grumbling. If it changes back, don't be surprised; if it stays the same, don't be surprised; if the committees turn it into ten species, don't be surprised—but do race home to update your lists, because you will have just gotten nine new birds, and all for free.

In the spring, males have lots of black; in the winter, males found in California are more muted. Always they have a dab of yellow at the base of their tails.

Small and active, kinglets (below) join warbler flocks. Note the small bill and two wing bars.

Townsend's Warbler *Setophaga townsendi*

👀 coastal forests (and deserts in migration)

A foggy winter morning with the dew dripping off the trees gets a jolt of chrome yellow when flocks of these warblers move through, often joined by kinglets, chickadees, and yellow-rumped warblers. Both females and males are green above, white below, with very snappy yellow-and-black face stripes, a pattern that is made even more jaunty by the small Nike swoosh under the eye. The classic warbler bill shows us it does not eat seeds but instead hunts spiders, moths, beetles, and caterpillars. In flight, outer tail feathers flash white.

Most Townsend's warblers head to Alaska and the Pacific Northwest in summer, breeding in spruce and Douglas fir. On the southbound loop some migrate as far as Costa Rica, and some stop over in Mexico, but many winter in the California lowlands, with a notable concentration in Monterey. Winter chip notes are sharp, metallic, and enticing: hearing *tzik tzik* reminds us to look up, since a warbler flock is somewhere nearby.

On their breeding grounds they stick to the tops of the conifers, but in migration and in winter they can be found feeding low in bushes, at mid-canopy in streamside alders, or in the crowns of eucalyptus trees. They tolerate urban habitats and can be found in coastal city parks and well-planted backyards. On average they prefer pines and spruces, and on average they stay west of the Sierra Crest, other than a small spike of spring migration through the Mojave Desert. The only thing better than spotting a winter flock of Townsend's warblers is to find a cottonwood tree in the desert filled with Townsend's, Wilson's, yellow, black-throated gray, and hermit warblers—and sometimes even the odd stray or two, like an American redstart or the East Coast's black-and-white warbler.

John Kirk Townsend was a mid-nineteenth-century naturalist and explorer who—like Cassin of Cassin's kingbird fame—died from arsenic poisoning, an early hazard when preparing specimen after specimen.

A thousand warbling echoes have started to life within me.
—Walt Whitman

Spotted Towhee *Pipilo maculatus*

It is a mix of expected attributes, this one. And so: seed-eater, favors brushy slopes and thickets of chaparral, hard to see, male only comes into the open when it sings, must be stalked quietly and patiently—yes, darn it, we've seen this list before. Even the spotted towhee's back-and-forth scratching hop is also used by California towhees and other sparrows. It would be nice if it had some special bling, like white horns or a tutti-frutti beak, or a special talent, like burping purple gas. Instead, it acts like lots of other birds. From pickup trucks to a basic coffee cup, some designs just can't be made better.

Smaller than a robin and bigger than all the other sparrows, its black back and chestnut sides (and red eye, if you're close enough) help you know that it is the spotted towhee you're looking at and not anything else. The black-headed grosbeak has a much heftier bill and is most often in the trees, not scritchy-scratchying under bushes. In fact the spotted towhee used to be called the rufous-sided towhee—a helpful and accurate name—but in a taxonomic revision a few years ago, it got peeled off from its eastern half, and each side of the pair got assigned new names to go with their new range maps.

A related family member in mountain meadows is called the green-tailed towhee (even though the first thing you notice is usually the reddish beanie cap), and again, as there is with the California thrasher and crissal thrasher, there's an all-brown outlier towhee at the bottom end of the Salton Sea, Abert's towhee.

The spotted towhee used to be called the rufous-sided towhee, a name some birders still use.

California Towhee   *Melozone crissalis*

The California towhee takes a moment to appreciate. Plain as a heel of bread, there's none of the drama that nature shows train us to expect: no sharp talons, no screaming power dives, not even an edge-of-extinction backstory.

Instead, this bird models utility and blending in. Towhees make their living hopping and scratching, looking for seeds and insects and hanging out in the shadows. Their color is the plainest of browns top to bottom, with a subtle glow of nutmeg under the tail. Yet they have the quiet grace of Shaker furniture. These large bush-sparrows are unpretentious, modest, and willing to make do with the basics—seeds, beetles, and the berries from chaparral plants like poison oak—and for that we should admire them. They can be found on the edges of deserts and forests, and in brushland or on college campuses. They certainly don't mind parks and backyards; the photos on this page were all taken near the middle of a city.

At the end of Jonathan Franzen's novel *Purity,* the main character, Pip, meditates on the birds of the Santa Cruz Mountains. Spending a rainy winter in a cabin, Pip notes that towhees are "a perfect medium size, more substantial than juncos, more modest than jays." The towhee's striking, monosyllabic chip note is usually transcribed as *teeek* or *zeeek*. That spelling doesn't capture its bright sharpness: Franzen compares the call to the squeak of a sneaker on the basketball court. Others think it sounds like the *chirp chirp* of a low-battery smoke detector. These birds live near—and have the same high-pitched alarm bark as—California ground squirrels, another native of weedy fields and quotidian brush. Hearing the scolding note from either bird or squirrel reminds us to look up. Is there a hawk we're about to miss, or is it our own clomping presence that has them so riled up?

Beauty is not just about aesthetics; it is a way of looking at the world that values things we can't put a material price on.

—Fiona Reynolds

Lark Sparrow *Chondestes grammacus*

👀 fields, woodland edges, open country (including deserts)

Quail-head, road-bird, lark-finch: maybe it has so many folk names because nobody can believe such a well-marked bird is just a sparrow. The "lark" part of the name honors the cheerful, lark-like song. Ground nesters and ground feeders, lark sparrows will flock even in nesting season, sorting through grass and gravel for seeds, seeds, grasshoppers, and seeds. They prefer open country—parks, rangeland, brushy deserts—yet come into the city if there's enough open space, including the Presidio in San Francisco or the Baldwin Hills above Culver City.

Let's take it from the top: the crown has a white stripe, then below that is a thick chestnut stripe, then below that is a tan stripe, then the eye itself has a white crescent and a thin black line from beak to ear, then below that is a chestnut swoosh, then another white stripe, then a wedge of black, then the white throat. The tail is brown but with bold white edges, visible as bright flashes when it flies or lands. That the in-between part (body, chest, wings) is just a regular, plain ole sparrow brown feels like a bit of a relief—the pause between crescendos. Its black chest dot might be a helpful field mark, if the head didn't already steal the show.

Common in California in every season (mostly west of the Sierra crest, and in the lower deserts), this bird is migratory in the rest of the Lower 48, moving from the high prairies down to Texas, Florida, and Mexico for the winter. If you've ever looked at a weather map for North Dakota in January, it will be obvious why. Humans hitch up their Airstreams and follow them south as well—earning them the name "snowbirds." Sparrows and humans alike might better be called *anti*-snow birds, common-sense birds, or, even more truthfully, mimosas-and-huevos-rancheros-for-Sunday-brunch birds.

Why fight when you can negotiate?
—Captain Jack Sparrow

Song Sparrow *Melospiza melodia*

👀 wet, brushy meadows and parks

Stare with your ears.—Ken Nordine

Although they do sing well and loudly and from visible perches, song sparrows stick mostly to the wettest, shrubbiest, most tangled places—marsh edges, brushy parks, Sierra meadows, willow forests, desert wetlands. Their range is expanding and they can be found higher in the Sierra than ever before. From the Aleutians to Newfoundland, twenty-five subspecies fill out the North American map, with three unique forms adapted to a saline lifestyle found in California salt marshes. For them, wet means *really* wet.

A streaky, stripy ground bird, it feeds low, usually coming into view if you wait patiently and quietly. A mix of gray and brown stripes, one thing that helps us ID a song sparrow is the way the lines on the chest almost always coalesce into a dark central spot. Resident California birds are joined by out-of-state cousins in winter, so you're bound to see some variation. We have a lot of wetland skulkers, including a smaller look-alike, the Lincoln's sparrow, and one with a yellow smudge by its eyes, the savannah sparrow, but habitat plus chest spot equals this species 99 times out of 100.

The species name *melodia* means just that, melodious, but yet again we have the gap between what the bird does (trills and rills, buzzes and warbles) and what our language accommodates (not much of anything: how would you even transcribe that *sppifff* when you open a can of soda?). Thoreau thought that song sparrows said, "Maids! Maids! Maids! Hang up your tea kettle-ettle-ettle." That's fine, but maybe a modern version would be "Dudes, dudes, dudes, surf's up, hurry, don't miss the shuttle-uttle-uttle."

En route to the nest, the bird with a mouth full of insects (top middle) reminds us how much protein seed-eating birds need to raise young.

White-crowned Sparrow · *Zonotrichia leucophrys*

👓 woodland and meadow edges, parks, yards

Mostly in flocks, mostly in winter, mostly everywhere that is park-like and shrubby, that's the main story here, plus the fact that most flocks contain a mix of ages and hence a mix of color patterns. Junco-sized and gregarious, adults have cleanly alternating black and white stripes, making them a snap to name, but immatures only have a basic brown-and-tan head pattern that resembles a number of options, turning them into contestants in the world's most boring game show, *Guess That Sparrow*. Luckily an adult almost always hops into view, wrapping up that episode, at least for now.

In summer most white-crowned sparrows migrate north to nest, but we do have one group that returns to the high country to breed in brush-edged meadows in the Sierra, as well as in a few forests farther south. Winter is our white-crowned sparrow season, and the birds can be found on or near the ground in parks, gardens, chaparral, marsh edges, and desert scrub, usually abundantly.

There is a second sparrow of the same size to consider, the golden-crowned sparrow, which only differs in having (wait for it) gold versus white top hats. They winter in Southern California but should be expected more commonly from Monterey north; it's much easier to see one in Golden Gate Park than it is in San Diego's Balboa Park, and easier too to find them along the coast than in the foothills. Golden-crowned sparrows breed in Alaska but share their song with us here: *Oh, dear meee.*

Study enough flocks of golden-crowned and white-crowned sparrows and sure enough an odd, third one will stand out: the eastern US's white-throated sparrow looks like a white-crowned one but has a white chin and a little flourish of yellow right before the eye. They don't really belong here, but each winter a few stray into view up and down the state. If they're around, rare bird alerts will spread the word.

I've chosen birds and fish, the creatures whose logic I wish to learn and live.
—Jim Harrison

In winter, golden-crowned sparrows (left) join flocks of white-crowneds.

Still on wintering grounds, a male (above) practices his song for when he arrives on territory, probably in Alaska.

Dark-eyed Junco *Junco hyemalis*

🔭 forests, woodland edges, parks, yards

Small sparrows with stubby, pale bills and (usually) dark heads, juncos are predominantly mountain birds in summer and, at least for some flocks, lowland birds in winter, generally sticking to forests or forest-habitat replacements, like cemeteries and suburban backyards. This is a flocking species, almost always found in groups. They hop on the ground or investigate low branches until a cat or hawk or sudden movement puts them into flight, and then you can see the bold white edges on the tail. (One assumes the white serves to startle a leaping predator and simultaneously to warn nearby

*I always felt like a bird blown through the world.
I never felt like a tree.—May Swenson*

songbirds.) The overall effect is one of being quite dapper. It is easy to agree with the poet William Stafford, who says, "Juncos...I like their / clean little coveralls."

They do make energetic use of bird feeders, and around campgrounds they will sometimes become familiar with people, hopping so close you can get a picture with your phone. They do well to stick close to us: more or less everything wants to eat them (or raid their nests), from daytime owls to weasels to snakes to a small falcon called a merlin. Some evidence indicates males winter farther north than females, presumably to be on site to breed as quickly as spring allows.

"Dark-eyed" not because they are sad-eyed ladies of the lowlands but to distinguish them from Arizona's yellow-eyed juncos, the name is an infinite bag of holding for many variously shaded populations; in California most juncos are the so-called Oregon form, latte-drinking and hip, but there also are slate-colored groups, white-winged groups, and the so-called pink-sided groups (which are more buff than pink). "Junco" as a term comes from *juncus*, the Latin word for reed, which is the one habitat you won't ever find them in. What can we say? Sometimes bird names, as with so many things in life, make no sense at all.

Western Tanager   *Piranga ludoviciana*

👀 forests, woodlands (and parks in migration)

All birds are created equal, but some birds are more equal than others. When it comes to western tanagers, spring males win all the design awards. It is hard to top such a perfectly spiced mix of yellow, orange-red, and black, with yellow blazes added to black wings. Poet May Swenson calls this bird "fireface," and it's also the symbol of the Los Angeles Audubon Society.

I hope you love birds too. It is economical. It saves going to Heaven.
—Emily Dickinson

This is a forest-nesting, treetop-foraging bird that either visits us briefly from its true home in Mexico and Costa Rica or else we can think of it as an essential part of the California avifauna that nips south only during the coldest, leanest parts of the year. Either way, it moves north in April and May, turning up in a wide variety of lowland parks and gardens and residential neighborhoods and woodland lots; then in high summer it breeds in the conifers of coastal and Sierra mountains. They eat cicadas and caterpillars as well as fruit. Some western tanagers head south as early as late July, but the main push is September. Females are greeny yellow with yellow wing bars; immatures and females of the less-common summer tanager are just plain yellow, minus any wing bars. (Male summer tanagers are the only large all-red birds in the woods, but their population is confined to belts of riparian cottonwood forest. The Lower Kern River is one place to look.)

The term "tanager" covers a group of almost three hundred species, mostly centered in South America; the word itself comes from a South American tribal language. Sometimes in spring migration you'll come across a bush or tree just exploding with western tanagers, and when that happens, no matter how early your day started or how much you spent on binoculars, you're bound to say, "I'm so glad I got up this morning."

Females and immature males (right) can be hard to tell apart, but a spring male (above) always stands out.

Black-headed Grosbeak Pheucticus melanocephalus

 woodlands, brushy edges (and parks in migration)

Blame the French for the strange name: "gros" as in the word for large, not as in repulsive or gross. And indeed, this orange-and-black mega-sparrow does have a very

The more you look, the more you will see.—Roger Tory Peterson

substantial, powerful beak. It can crack sunflower seeds lickety-split, making cabin owners think, "But I just filled that feeder an hour ago." Males add to the bold plumage with white wing bars and yellow underwings. In a pattern found often in the avian kingdom, females and young males are streakier and less vividly marked.

Mosaic habitats attract them: not uniform chaparral but edges, streams, understory, trees. Diet too varies: like very, very small bears, they mix it up, going equally for berries, seeds, fruit, and insects. Its sweet and musical song has been compared to the song of a drunk robin. (Do birds get drunk? Yes, if berries ferment on the bush.) Females sing too, generally with less complexity than the males, and as with other birds, these songs express availability for mating, claim territorial ownership, and, sometimes, reinforce pair bonding. The family that sings karaoke together stays together. They also call out *schick schick,* not to promote razors but to stay in contact when feeding in underbrush or dense woods.

This is generally a bird of the wide-open West, present April to September and shifting to Mexico for winter, where it overlaps with the eastern species, the rose-breasted grosbeak. In fall, a few grosbeaks linger in California, especially in desert oases, but they're just as likely to be the rose-breasted ones as the western kind. Why do those eastern grosbeaks fly all the way here instead of zipping down to Mexico? Presumably their orienteering skills are a bit off, or maybe they just hope to get a job in the movies.

Adult (left) and immature (above). Is "about the size of an orange" a good way to describe a bird?

Mobbing: The Little Guys Take on the Big Guys

Top: "We don't want your kind around here!"—western kingbirds dive-bomb a great horned owl.

Bottom: Red-winged blackbirds take on a red-tailed hawk.

To some birds, when they run into unwanted company the motto is *Anywhere but here*. For blackbirds it might be crows they can't abide, or for crows it might be red-tailed hawks. Mobbing is a behavior one sees in many bird groups up and down the list, and it means the little guys feint and strafe until the offending victim—the hawk or cat or raven or biologist—packs up and moves on. They don't usually peck hard enough to do harm, but like a cloud of mosquitoes, an angry mob of chickadees and warblers can harry an owl until it gives up and flies off.

Birders try to trigger this by pishing (slurring out the fussing, scolding alarm call of small birds; see page 123), but mobbing itself can alert us to a snake or owl we might otherwise miss. Once you watch for it, you'll see it happens all the time, even right over downtown freeways.

We have mixed feelings about group bullying in our own culture. A crowd's fury can topple the Berlin Wall, but that same kind of crowd can turn into a lynch mob very quickly. Does too much humanity all in one place cause madness? Thomas Hardy thought so, titling his novel *Far from the Madding Crowd*. "To mad" is an archaic verb similar to "madden"—and many hawks know that feeling well. Beware the wrath of the little guys.

Red-winged Blackbird *Agelaius phoeniceus*

👀 marshes, reedy lakes, wet fields, parks

If they could do wheelies and shoot flames from their bike spokes, they would. Male red-winged blackbirds puff their red shoulders and lean forward from perches, insisting so hard on their territorial claims one worries their eyes will bug right out of their heads. Does it work? Less than they may hope; though a loud and bossy male may have a harem of fifteen resident females, genetics reveal that plenty of the eggs were sired by somebody else.

Red-winged blackbirds are a touch smaller than robins. They are widespread and colonial, and continent-wide they may total 250 million birds. They eat grain and insects. The male is glossy black and sharp-billed, with red-and-yellow shoulder patches and a wide, rounded tail. The thin band of yellow varies and can be hard to see, but the red epaulette brightly advertises macho status whether the bird is perched or in flight. Females have no red, just tan eyestripes and heavily streaked brown bodies. The textbook blackbird habitat is a cattail marsh or flooded field, but if that's not possible, then a catchment basin, sewage pond, feedlot, or just the parking lot of Burger King will do.

They can make a lot of noise, but we have to be honest: this bird's gargling, gurgling *conk-guh-REE* song sounds about as seductive as Gollum playing the bugle. It could be worse: when it comes to the two sister species, the yellow-headed blackbird's song sounds like somebody forcing open a door with a bad hinge, and the tricolored blackbird sounds like somebody trying to strangle a cat. Of course to them, they probably would think Frank

Sinatra sounds too bland; more to their taste might be Bob Dylan on a bad night.

He who sings scares away his woes.—Miguel de Cervantes

Red on black could make a really snappy superhero costume.

Another marsh blackbird, the yellow-headed (above) has an all-white wing flash.

Western Meadowlark *Sturnella neglecta*

Recipe for happiness: a pasture or short-grass prairie or marshy field, a fence post or waist-high snag, sunrise, and a meadowlark cued up and ready to yodel its heart out. It's robin-sized but more stout and very, very electric yellow, with pink legs and a V for victory Sharpied onto its breast in deep, indelible black. When it cocks its head back and lets go with its full song cycle, hang on with both hands because this will be a soaring mix of trills, warbles, and flutey whistles; and when it stops there's a different song that follows, and another after that, carrying on past ten or twelve. No wonder six different states count it as their official state bird. (That does raise the question, though, of whether multiple states should be allowed to claim the same bird. Perhaps whoever gets the meadowlark first is the winner and the next state has to pick a new emblem. Ladybugs are really popular state mascots too, as are cardinals.)

The yellow and black combo makes this a bird you can spot from a quarter mile away. Yet if you flip the coin, this is a bird that can disappear as soon it stops singing and drops down into the dry grass. Profile-altering face stripes and a checkered blend of black-edged tans create a highly functional cloak of invisibility; the back half of the plumage is so cryptic you can know exactly where the bird landed yet still not find it. That is irritatingly true about lots of birds out in nature (instead of watching them in an aviary at the zoo). Of course, they have had millions of years to perfect their hide-and-seek choices, while most of us have only been birdwatching for fifty or sixty years, max, and usually a lot less.

There's an eastern meadowlark as well—identical colors, different voice—but it comes no closer to us than southeastern Arizona. And so yellow breast, black V, great song cycle, and zero look-alikes in our area—bingo. With the western meadowlark, we just about have the perfect combination.

The ultimate skill is noticing.—*Marcel Proust*

Brewer's Blackbird   *Euphagus cyanocephalus*

👀 meadows, parks, lawns, towns

If anybody ever wants to do a micro-tweet summary of California birds, Brewer's blackbirds will be easy: "Black body, pale eye, loves lawns and meadows." The male's ivory-white eye is so bright and round it looks sewn on; female Brewer's blackbirds are plainer, browner, and darker-eyed. (Female red-winged blackbirds are always streakier than this species.) Males sometimes attack their own reflections in the side mirrors of cars.

When settling the plains, pioneers used to claim "rain follows the plow." Meteorology doesn't work that way, but we could say, "Blackbirds follow the road crews." Originally this was a Sierra meadow bird, expected at Lake Tahoe or Tioga Pass, and it still can be found there, especially around campgrounds and horse trails. But now the Brewer's blackbird is just as likely to be noticed far away from the Sierra meadows at a fast-food place or an I-5 rest stop, joining house sparrows to check for crumbs under the picnic tables, or perhaps hopping up to peck dead insects from the front of car grilles. Yards, parks, streams, stables, shopping centers, golf courses, grassy cemeteries—all strike it as equally suitable—and while one most often expects to see it directly on the grass or cement, they also forage (and roost) in trees. Food is a mix of seeds and grasses, plus insects in summer.

Irrigation of the land with seawater desalinated by fusion power is ancient. It's called rain.
—Mike McAlary

Identification is easy so long as the twice-as-big great-tailed grackle is considered and discarded: the two have similar colors but very different shapes, sizes, and vocal patterns. When morning light hits a male Brewer's blackbird it's as if somebody announced "Show-time!" and flicked on a switch. Plain and puritanical black suddenly incandesces into purples, blues, greens. The eye looks even more striking then, and the entire bird looks brighter, larger, more newly minted.

Thomas Mayo Brewer was a nineteenth-century naturalist who also has a desert sparrow named after him. His father took part in the Boston Tea Party.

Females (left) are plainer and browner; males (above) have bright yellow eyes and glossy, all-black coloring.

Great-tailed Grackle *Quiscalus mexicanus*

👓 parks, reedy lakeshores, towns

Coming to a parking lot near you: a huge blackbird with a parade-float tail and a voice like truck brakes worn right down to the metal. Native originally to the thickets and jungles of Texas and Mexico south to Panama, this once was a rare bird in California. Starting at the Salton Sea and flowing up each side of the Sierra, it has steadily spread north, favoring city parks, reedy lakes, and parking lots, until now grackles can be found from San Diego to San Francisco, and sometimes all the way north to the Oregon border.

Bigger than any other all-black bird except ravens and crows, a grackle looks different from a crow—more stretched out, with a rudder-shaped tail that looks like it got glued on sideways. The iridescent black males are larger and noisier than the brown-and-tan females. Both sexes have pale eyes and offer a shopping spree of noises, from rattles, trills, and chuckles to long, screechy whistles that sound like R2-D2 teaching naughty words to dolphins.

In winter at that house rowdy grackles shook out their feathers, black and shiny as the skin of night rivers, and gathered in the skeletons of winter trees.—Sandra Cisneros

Grackles eat more or less everything, and they can be quite adroit at finding lizards, spiders, bird eggs, and day-old french fries. Yet they'll raid crops too, piercing fruit to suck out the soft pulp, or scarfing up all the grain in a field. Many farmers curse them as pests, and it's easy to see why.

Abundant in the urban tropics, this may be the first species you see when you get out of the plane on your birdwatching vacation to Costa Rica. Great-tailed grackles are expanding their range north at 2.5 percent a year, so for better or worse, if it's not on your yard list yet, it probably will be soon.

Males are darker, bigger, louder; females browner, smaller, quieter.

Hooded Oriole *Icterus cucullatus*

👀 palm trees in towns and deserts

Men argue. Nature acts.—Voltaire

Hooded orioles arrive in March, our northern ambassadors from the tropics and the sunny deserts. They stay through midsummer to drink nectar and eat insects, nest in palms, and generally crank the fun meter to 11. By August the males have turned south again, followed in September by the females and juveniles. It is a brief season, but while they are here, *¡Qué fabuloso!* Spring males glow with a throbbing yellow so saturated you wonder how the missus sleeps at night.

The shape is typically "oriolene" (or perhaps one should say "icteridish"), meaning it has a slender body, a sharp and elongated bill, and a long tail. All male orioles show bright colors, usually contrasted with black, and the hooded oriole fits this pattern exactly. The "hood" is the orange cowl that is set off by the black back, black wings, and black face and bib. Females are plainer, calmer, with a greener hue and no black contrasts. Nests are woven sacks sort of like long socks, and anchored to the same palm fronds they are sewn from.

Thanks to the widespread planting of palm trees, hooded orioles are more common than ever before. Historically it was a bird of streams and desert oases, but now it has become a backyard bird all over urban Southern California, nesting all the way up to San Francisco. They can be seen in Arcata—far from fan palm oases in Joshua Tree and Palm Springs—and even in Bishop. One very brave (or very lost) hooded oriole even has made it to Juneau, Alaska.

For orioles and other semitropical birds, yards are a two-part gift. We've not just added a palmy, overwatered lushness to the urban landscape, but we also invented these crazy fountains called hummingbird feeders, and orioles really dig them. A few like California so much they spend the winter here, perhaps the advance guard for a second invasion, one of year-round orioles. Of course, if orioles ever start overwintering in Anchorage, we will finally have to admit climate change is for real.

Feral fan palms in the bed of the L.A. River.

Appendix I: Further Resources

Get hooked on birds and you'll need a new bookshelf. There are surveys of the birds of other countries, monographs on specialty groups like seabirds, and regional guides for the different parts of the US. There is a great bird book devoted to the High Sierra, and there are breeding bird surveys organized by county. Once, when I was moving, I labeled my boxes, and a too-tall stack of them were tagged *bird books*. Helping to Sherpa the endless load into the house, a friend decided enough was enough. He set them on the sidewalk and went on strike. "Nobody should own this many bird books."

When you are ready to go past the basics, these five titles will help. All are great.

The first is the companion book to this one, Matt Ritter's *A Californian's Guide to the Trees among Us*. If you are curious about the history of the eucalyptus in California or want to know where pepper trees come from, it's a fun book laid out like this one.

For birds, there are two national guides and two regional ones to look for. Both national books feature painted plates, not photographs. All owe an infinite debt to Roger Tory Peterson, whose 1934 *Guide to the Birds* sold out in one week, even though it was published in the middle of the Depression. All field guide authors hope to achieve his succinct clarity.

For supplements to this book, first among equals is the *National Geographic Field Guide to the Birds of North America* by Jon L. Dunn and Jonathan Alderfer. If you want the continent-wide overview from the Aleutians to Key West, this surprisingly compact, deeply authoritative field guide contains an entry for every bird in the U.S.A. and Canada. (Hawai'i is not usually included in any of the North American field guides, nor is Mexico.) There is an app version of this book that's very strong as well, and it includes many birdsong recordings.

David Allen Sibley's *Sibley Guide to Birds* has a larger page size and more information on subspecies and local color variations; his book is a tribute to his skill as a painter and his ability to notice subtle details. Some think it's a bit heavy for field use and keep it as a backup in the car; others won't go anywhere without tossing it in the backpack.

Two state books are both photo-illustrated. Alvaro Jaramillo is a naturalist based in Half Moon Bay, and his book, the *American Birding Association Field Guide to Birds of California*, came out in 2015 and features three hundred species.

Kimball Garrett works for the Natural History Museum of Los Angeles County and partnered with Jon Dunn (author of the *National Geographic Field Guide,* above) to release a very compact book, *Birds of Southern California*. Its scope is broader than the title indicates, and it makes a good companion to Jaramillo's book. Both titles feature photos by Brian E. Small.

A list of all wild birds of California can be found online by searching the California Bird Records Committee with the keywords "Official California Checklist." As we go to print, the state total is 673.

Appendix II: eBird and Electronic Resources

In the dark ages before the Internet, to create the first list of birds for UC Irvine's San Joaquin Marsh I had to be a detective, anthropologist, and clairvoyant. I interviewed octogenarian duck hunters, checked specimens in museum collections, reviewed mimeographed bird club reports, bugged strangers for their field notes, and tagged along on biological surveys. I studied old photos and heard tales about when the most essential tool for birdwatching in Orange County was a shovel—to dig out your jeep when trespassing on muddy ranch roads. The final document was designed using an IBM Selectric typewriter and proofread by the English department's part-time secretary.

Welcome to the future. A blend of citizen science, crowdsourcing, and communal goodwill, the eBird database allows you to review sightings with magical ease. You can find out what people saw at Lake Merritt in Oakland yesterday or monitor spring migrants more broadly. Using eBird you can find out that Orange County's Huntington Central Park has a master list of 306 birds and that 1,600 daily checklists have been posted. You can look at bar graphs, compare high counts, study photos of rarities, and even get driving directions.

To begin using it, go to ebird.org (free and no registration needed), then go to "Explore Data," then "Explore Hotspots," and zoom in on the part of the map you want to investigate. Look for red circles: those locations have the most sightings. You can filter activity by date to narrow the results. Smartphones of course help in getting observations updated quickly, and this aggregate of data has great potential to reveal trends and document bird populations.

It's also fun just to let your imagination run free—so what *is* happening in Kenya this week? In Nairobi National Park somebody saw twenty-five ostriches yesterday and a flock of oxpeckers. In Yellowstone it was a good day for pileated woodpeckers. With eBird you can become the ultimate flâneur, with the entire world as your boulevard.

Oliver W., the famous trotting ostrich at Florida Ostrich Farm, Jacksonville. Detroit Publishing Co., ca. 1903.

A Note on Photography

All the photos but two were taken of birds in the wild, usually (but not always) in California. The one captive bird is shown on pages 2 and 49: the tufted puffin. It was a rehab bird photographed in Alaska. Most photos were shot digitally, with a few brought into the book from the slide era, scanned and converted for publication. By coincidence, author Charles Hood and photographer Callyn Yorke both shoot on Nikon cameras, but all the brands these days are equally good.

Acknowledgments

Thank you to Eve Bachrach, Bruce Bartrug, Peter Bowler, Bonnie Brady, Bill Bretz, Kevin Bryan, Jared Burton, Scott Covell, Jack Cull, Briony Everroad, Kelly Fernandez, Mama Fitting, Raymond Fitting, Andrea Fonville, Deb Ford, Bill Fox, Sara Frantz, Jonathan Franzen, Kristin Friedrich, Joan Fry, Kimball Garrett, Wendy Gilmartin, Charles Goodrich, Keith Hansen, John Haubrich, Richard Hayden, Lila Higgins, Mark Hoffer, Abbey Hood, Amber Hood, Fred Hood, David Jackson, Matthew Jaffe, Roger Linfield, Chet McGaugh, Todd Newberry, Greg Pauly, PLAYA Arts Foundation, Matthew Rainbow, Trudy Siptroth, Bill Vaughn, Patricia Wakida, Gayle Wattawa, and Cal Yorke.

Index

Crowley Lake 59
Cuba 37
Culver City 130
curlew, long-billed 9, 44, 46

D

Dakotas, the 30, 45, 130
Darwin (town) 32
Darwin, Charles 31, 66, 116
DDT 60, 70, 75, 84
Death Valley National Park 8, 9, 32, 112
dipper, American 111
diver, great northern 6
Doty, Mark 102
dove, Eurasian collared- 11, 32, 33
dove, mourning 5, 32, 33, 72
dove, spotted 32
duck, Muscovy 20
duck, mutt 20
duck, ruddy 25
duck, wood 19
dunlin 9, 45
Dunn, Jon 143

E

eagle, bald 2, 9, 69, 70, 75
eagle, golden 68, 70, 74, 75, 102
eBird 145
egret, cattle 63
egret, great 12, 61, 62, 63
egret, snowy 63, 66, 145
El Niño 50, 55
Eliot, T.S. 101
emu 4
endemic 2, 75, 95
Exposition Park 104
Eureka 32

F

falcon, peregrine 83, 84, 117
Farallon Islands 2, 49
finch, Cassin's 121
finch, house 72, 121
finch, purple 121
finch, spice 119
flamingo, American 66
flicker, northern 4, 82
flicker, red-shafted 82
Florida 6, 69, 85, 87, 130
flycatcher, vermilion 13, 89, 90, 119
Franzen, Jonathan 129
Fresno 106

G

gadwall 14
Garrett, Kimball 38, 109, 143
Getty Villa 86
godwit, marbled 45, 46, 84
Golden Gate Bridge 2, 49, 103, 114
Golden Gate Park 39, 65, 106, 132
goldfinch, American 5, 122
goldfinch, Lawrence's 122
goldfinch, lesser 122
Goodrich, Charles 96
goosander 6
goose, brant 18
goose, Canada 17, 18, 25
goose, Ross's 17
goose, snow 17
grackle, great-tailed 140
Grand Canyon 35, 68
Great Basin 4, 75
grebe, Clark's 29, 30
grebe, eared 29
grebe, pied-billed 29
grebe, western 29, 30
grosbeak, black-headed 128, 135
grosbeak, rose-breasted 135
gull, California 51, 53
gull, glaucous-winged 52
gull, Heermann's 50, 55
gull, herring 52
gull, ring-billed 51
gull, Western 11, 51, 52, 54, 145
gull, yellow-footed 52

H

Hahamongna Park 81
Half Moon Bay 23, 48, 55
Hammon Grove Park 8
harrier, northern 71
Hart Park 87
Hass, Robert 92
Hawai'i 2, 119, 127
hawk, chicken 72
hawk, Cooper's 72, 88, 117
hawk, duck 84
hawk, marsh 71
hawk, red-shouldered 73
hawk, red-tailed 74, 79, 136
hawk, sharp-shinned 72
hawk, sparrow 83
hawk, zone-tailed 67
Hearst Castle 57
Heermann, Adolphus 50
Hemet 37, 65
heron, goliath 61
heron, great blue 15, 61

heron, grey 61
heronries 66
Highway 1 57, 84
Highway 99 96
Hollywood 72, 110
Hopkins, Gerard Manley 83
Houston 119
Humboldt Bay 18
Humboldt State University 3
hummingbird, Allen's 36, 37
hummingbird, Anna's 36, 37, 38
hummingbird, bee 37
hummingbird, black-chinned 36
hummingbird, ruby-throated 36
Huntington Gardens 86
Huntington Beach Central Park 144

I

I-5 3, 74, 139
ibis, glossy 65
ibis, sacred 65
ibis, white-faced 28, 65
Iceland 22
Iran 22

J

Jaramillo, Alvaro 143
jay, blue 80, 94
jay, brown 94
jay, California scrub- 94, 95
jay, gray 94
jay, green 94
jay, magpie- 94
jay, pinyon 4, 94
jay, Steller's 93
Joshua Tree National Park 8, 141
junco, dark-eyed 72, 102, 129, 133
junco, yellow-eyed 133
Juneau 141

K

Kea 85
Kern County 90
kestrel, American 4, 83
killdeer 43, 46, 84
King City 78
kingbird, Cassin's 91
kingbird, western 13, 89, 91, 136
kingfisher, belted 13
kinglet 103, 127
kiwi 4
Klamath Basin 28

L

La Jolla 32, 57
Laguna Beach 48
Laguna Mountains 106
Lake Merritt 58, 144
Lake Tahoe 3, 139
Las Vegas 36
Lee Vining 100
Lewis, Meriwether 30, 68
little brown job (LBJ) 13
London 87
Long Beach 48
loon, common 6, 30
Los Angeles 11, 35, 68, 85, 86, 90, 103,
    104, 106
Los Angeles Audubon Society 134
Los Angeles County 3, 119
Los Angeles River 3, 9, 40, 58, 65, 69, 86,
    87, 141

M

magpie, black-billed 95
magpie, yellow-billed 2, 95
Maine 32
Malibu Lagoon 14, 23
mallard 20, 21, 22, 23
manikin 119
Marin County 103
Masséna, Anna 36
Maya mythology 86
meadowlark, eastern 30, 138
meadowlark, western 30, 138
merganser 6
merganser, hooded 24
merlin 72, 133
Mexico 17, 20, 21, 37, 60, 69, 85, 101,
    116, 127, 130, 134, 135, 140
Mission San Juan Capistrano 100
mobbing 110, 136
mockingbird, northern 88, 92, 116
Mono Lake 51, 53, 58, 59, 69, 99
Monterey 42, 52, 55, 57, 84, 103, 127, 132
Morro Bay 18
Morro Rock 84
Mount Diablo 50
Mount Whitney 8
Muir, John 68, 111
Muir Woods 108, 114
munia, scaly-breasted 14, 119
murre, common 49

S

T

U

University of California 73, 74, 95, 104
Utah 53, 91

V

Ventura County 119
verdin 104, 109
Virgil 101
Visalia 87
vulture, black 67
vulture, turkey 5, 67, 68, 74

W

warbler, Audubon's 126
warbler, black-and-white 127
warbler, black-throated gray 127
warbler, hermit 127
warbler, MacGillivray's 12
warbler, myrtle 126
warbler, Townsend's 127
warbler, Wilson's 125, 127
warbler, yellow 123, 125, 127
warbler, yellow-rumped 110, 126, 127
water ouzel 111
waxwing, cedar 118
West Nile virus 95
whimbrel 44, 46, 84
whip-poor-will 110
Whitman, Walt 78
willet 48
wind turbines 75
woodpecker, acorn 81
wren, Bewick's 108
wren, cactus 104, 109
wren, canyon 108
wren, house 108, 110
wren, marsh 107, 108, 124
wren, Pacific 108

Y

Yellowstone 35, 144
yellowthroat, common 124
Yosemite 3, 8, 58, 59, 72, 81, 84, 100, 106,
     111, 124
Yucatán 100

Z

Zzyzx 3

About the Author

Charles Hood has studied birds and natural history from the Amazon to Tibet, and he has seen more than five thousand species of birds in the wild. A widely published poet, he has received numerous fellowships and writing awards, and his most recent artist-in-residence positions were with the National Science Foundation in Antarctica and with PLAYA Arts in Oregon. He has also been a visiting professor in England, Mexico, and Papua New Guinea. Hood is currently a research fellow with the Center for Art + Environment at the Nevada Museum of Art, as well as a teacher of writing and photography at Antelope Valley College, in the Mojave Desert.

HEYDAY
into California

About Heyday

Heyday is an independent, nonprofit publisher and unique cultural institution. We promote widespread awareness and celebration of California's many cultures, landscapes, and boundary-breaking ideas. Through our well-crafted books, public events, and innovative outreach programs we are building a vibrant community of readers, writers, and thinkers.

Thank You

It takes the collective effort of many to create a thriving literary culture. We are thankful to all the thoughtful people we have the privilege to engage with. Cheers to our writers, artists, editors, storytellers, designers, printers, bookstores, critics, cultural organizations, readers, and book lovers everywhere!

We are especially grateful for the generous funding we've received for our publications and programs during the past year from foundations and hundreds of individual donors. Major supporters include:

Anonymous; Arkay Foundation; Judith and Phillip Auth; Judy Avery; Richard and Rickie Ann Baum; Randy Bayard; BayTree Fund; Jean and Fred Berensmeier; Nancy Bertelsen; Edwin Blue; Philip and Jamie Bowles; Beatrice Bowles; Peter Boyer and Terry Gamble Boyer; Brandt-Hawley Law Group; John Briscoe; California Humanities; The Campbell Foundation; John and Nancy Cassidy; The Christensen Fund; Lawrence Crooks; Chris Desser and Kirk Marckwald; Steven Dinkelspiel; Frances Dinkelspiel and Gary Wayne; The Roy and Patricia Disney Family Foundation; Tim Disney; Patricia Dixon; Gayle Embrey; Richard and Gretchen Evans; Megan Fletcher, in honor of J.K. Dineen; Patrick Golden and Susan Overhauser; Wanda Lee Graves and Stephen Duscha; Whitney Green; Walter & Elise Haas Fund; Penelope Hlavac; Nettie Hoge; Michael Horn, in memory of Gary Horn; Humboldt Area Foundation; JiJi Foundation; Claudia Jurmain; Kalliopeia Foundation; Marty Krasney; Abigail Kreiss; Guy Lampard and Suzanne Badenhoop; Thomas Lockard and Alix Marduel; David Loeb; Judith Lowry-Croul and Brad Croul; Praveen Madan and Christin Evans; Joel Marcus; Malcolm and Rina Margolin; William, Karen, and John McClung; Michael McCone; Nion McEvoy and Leslie Berriman, in honor of Malcolm Margolin; Judy Mistelske-Anklam and William Anklam; Karen and Tom Mulvaney; National Wildlife Federation; The Nature Conservancy; Eddie Orton;

The Ralph M. Parsons Foundation; Alan Rosenus; The San Francisco Foundation; San Manuel Band of Mission Indians; Greg Sarris; Save the Redwoods League; Stanley Smith Horticultural Trust; Roselyne Swig; Tappan Foundation; Thendara Foundation; Michael and Shirley Traynor, in honor of Malcolm Margolin; The Roger J. and Madeleine Traynor Foundation; Al and Ann Wasserman; Sherry Wasserman and Clayton F. Johnson; Lucinda Watson; Peter Wiley and Valerie Barth; Mina Witteman; and Yocha Dehe Wintun Nation.

Board of Directors

Getting Involved

To learn more about our publications, our events, and other ways you can participate, please visit www.heydaybooks.com.